FEARLESSLY FLUENT FAST: LEARN YOUR NEXT LANGUAGE FAST LIKE A KID!

7 SIMPLE NEURO-LINGUISTIC HACKS TO SPEAK YOUR FOREIGN LANGUAGE IN 3 MONTHS

USE EVERYDAY ACTIVITIES & BUILD FLUENCY FAST LIKE CHILDREN!

RYAN JOHNSON

© **Copyright 2022, 2024 - All rights reserved.**

The content contained within this book may not be reproduced, duplicated, or transmitted without direct written permission from the author or the publisher.

Under no circumstances will any blame or legal responsibility be held against the publisher, or author, for any damages, reparation, or monetary loss due to the information contained within this book, either directly or indirectly.

Legal Notice:

This book is copyright protected. It is only for personal use. You cannot amend, distribute, sell, use, quote or paraphrase any part, or the content within this book, without the consent of the author or publisher.

Please note the information contained within this document is for educational and entertainment purposes only. All effort has been executed to present accurate, up-to-date, reliable, and complete information. No warranties of any kind are declared or implied. Readers acknowledge that the author is not engaged in the rendering of legal, financial, medical, or professional advice. The content within this book has been derived from various sources. Please consult a licensed professional before attempting any techniques outlined in this book.

By reading this document, the reader agrees that under no circumstances is the author responsible for any losses, direct or indirect, that are incurred as a result of the use of the information contained within this document, including, but not limited to, errors, omissions, or inaccuracies.

CONTENTS

FOREWORD

Learning a new language can be daunting for so many reasons.

I can go on and on about the struggles too: from all those websites with generalized phrases, the long list of vocabulary words you've written down 10 times every other month, to that one foreign film you watched in the language you want to learn. Believe me, after years of globetrotting around the world, interviewing people in different languages, testing, scientific research, and even personal experiences. I've seen and heard it all.

But do you know the folks who have no problem with learning languages?

Kids!

As adults, we learn languages in a completely different way from kids, and that's okay. But we have so much to learn from the little ones! When it comes to unleashing our potential, babies and toddlers have a wealth of wisdom to share with us. If we look a little closer at how they learn, we have the potential to learn new languages at lightning speed. All just by thinking like a baby!

And that is where we'll start.

This time, learning another language will happen more smoothly than you think. To learn fast and efficiently, you must start by learning how newborns, children & early learners all naturally apply their secret tactics. You'll learn how to improve your ability to retain new knowledge and become proficient in a foreign language by changing your whole perspective on the language learning process. Breathing in the culture and mastering tactics that go beyond just first-level basic phrases. Start learning the way we all were meant to, and then soon, you'll be the one translating a foreign language for your friends and family.

INTRODUCTION

So you're entering the world of foreign languages! You've had this craving to learn it for a while now, and you even took a crack at it a while back. You looked at a few websites here and there, bought some books off Amazon, started a vocabulary notebook, or even made numerous flashcards. You may have dedicated a good 15 to 20 minutes with Duo Lingo while you waited for your laundry to finish.

But two months later, you still can't get past basic greeting phrases, conversations about the weather, and what to order at a restaurant. Even worse, you have 30+ unread Due Lingo messages waiting for you each day, reminding you how much you're falling behind.

Why is it so hard to learn a new language?!

It's like we get this fire to tackle, let's say, Spanish, and sometimes we stick it out for a few months before we hit a plateau and that inspirational fire burns out.

I get it… I've been there… This is what's referred to as "The PDPM Cycle" of Perfectionism, Doubt, Procrastination & Motivation renewed all over again. Have you ever felt this way before?

Well, we are all right here with you!

Countless other foreign language enthusiasts hit their heads on the wall wondering why a child can do it but they cannot.

And that's actually the most fascinating part. A CHILD can learn multiple languages easier than an adult (Ertheo, 2018). Now when you think about it, kids have a lot of time on their hands, and they're surrounded by the target language almost every second of their life. It's almost as if they have no choice but to learn their native language. And they can manage an additional one without much trouble at all. Their brains are like sponges. They absorb every word. Whether it makes sense to them at that moment or not, they're taking it all in. They'll eventually repeat it back to you with the correct context too.

YOU can learn a new language using the same techniques a child utilizes.

This time won't be like the others.

Do any of these apply to you?

- You've been studying a particular language for many years but still haven't gone beyond the basic level.
- Worried that you might be too old to be learning a new language.
- Tried different methods like classes, apps, books, and videos, but you can't seem to progress.
- You don't have the money or time to live in a foreign country to fully immerse yourself in the language.

- You don't have a lot of people with whom you can practice the language.
- Some may not have a lot of time to study and pore over books and do homework.
- Getting frustrated with your plateau & slow progress with becoming fluent.

If you've answered yes to even one (or all...Lol) of these common issues with learning a new language, then it's probably time to change your strategy.

I want to introduce you to a whole new way of thinking about finally achieving fluency in another language.

Prepare to learn completely refreshing methods and strategies that will help you:

- Fluently pick up a language and make it stick.
- Understand how children are able to become FLUENT LIGHTNING-FAST.
- Acquire MULTIPLE languages simultaneously and discover how you can apply this to your own learning now.
- Mastering your MEMORY to feel comfortable and confidently fluent in your foreign language.
- Address mindsets that could be holding you back from language learning SUCCESS.
- Strategies and life-hacks that will change your life & SAVE TIME.
- Debunk myths about language learning.

We will also discover the latest in neuroscience & tips from those who have successfully mastered foreign languages as an adult.

Now let's venture through the seven groundbreaking ways of learning your next language fluently: Each chapter presents a new perspective that'll make this time around much different than before.

WHO IS RYAN JOHNSON?

I am a full-time Language Teacher / Husband / Father / Author / Public Speaker / Certified & Accredited NeuroLanguage Coach / Translator / Polyglot / Passionate World Traveler.

I speak multiple languages:

English, Chinese (中文), Spanish, Czech, and I'm currently learning French, Tagalog, Portuguese, Thai and Korean (한국) along with several Slavic-based languages like Polish, Ukrainian, Slovakian, and Russian.

As a child, I used to go on vacations with my family. During those trips, I never really learned any of the local languages aside from a few basic words (and let's be honest, I was too busy having fun).

However, on an extended visit to Asia as an adult, I began to realize how much I was missing out on by not understanding the native language. So I decided to start learning Chinese for real! And that habit continued with me even after I left the country to return home.

Learning one foreign language opened up a passion within me now for learning many different kinds of languages. It made me want to learn the various languages of the different people I met in my own city. I began that journey with the places I used to visit as a child.

I've applied what I learned from my University Studies in Applied Neuroscience along with my own research on this topic to become fluent in multiple languages. My passion grew so much that I even taught the languages to my students!

My credentials extend from my many years of experience mastering my craft to my University Degree in Education specializing in Language Acquisition & Applied Neuroscience, and my pure love of learning about different world maps, cultures & languages. I'm also a Trained Certified NeuroLanguage Coach accredited by the ICF (International Coach Federation).

With over 20 years of experience, I've been helping Native English Speakers to FLUENTLY SPEAK their Foreign Languages, achieving their own uniquely desired results. Now I want to help YOU master your target language and achieve fluency.

I understand how learning new languages can completely change your life and open up new worlds of opportunity to help you relate to other human beings on this earth who are different from you. This creates a positive impact and an outward ripple effect for us all across our green & blue marble. Because I have this understanding, I've applied and taught these very same fluency methods to many students who've become FEARLESSLY FLUENT FAST as adults.

So why write this book now? Well, over the years, many friends have begged me to share my secrets with the world. My life has been enriched by my personal travels, living in multiple countries and I've even boosted my career because of learning new languages. Now I want others to enjoy the fortunes and experience the joyous rewards that can open up for them by mastering their foreign language. That's why I decided to unlock my secrets and share them with you in such an intimate way, through this book. So here's to YOU my friend!

I BELIEVE IN YOU! 🩶

Happy language learning!

THINK LIKE A KID

 *"Language is to the mind more than light is to the eye."*

— WILLIAM GIBSON

Okay, let's talk about how these little polyglots learn a language!

Did you know that a baby starts learning their native tongue even before they're born? According to writer Stevie D. of FluentU - Foreign Language Immersion Online, babies have already begun learning their language from pre-birth (D, 2015).

It was widely assumed that language acquisition occurs after birth. Scientists in Washington, D.C., however, debunked that with some research.

They offered moms a tape of nonsense phrases to listen to over the last few weeks of their pregnancy. When within their mother's womb, the newborns heard the quasi words between 50-71 times. These newborns were tested shortly after Scientists could look at pictures of the newborns' brains while the fake phrases were played by connecting them to an EEG, and you know what they discovered? The newborns recalled and identified the words that were provided to them while they were still inside their mother's belly.

The unborn child was listening the whole time!

They discovered that day one of acquiring language doesn't exactly start when the baby is born. It starts 30 weeks during pregnancy. The baby grows ears and starts to listen to their world around them.

And of course, it doesn't stop there.

During the first year of life, a kid unwittingly builds up a mental picture bank of the things, emotions, and behaviors they describe. The typical number of words that a baby can comprehend by the end of their first year is between 10 and 50. Children begin speaking after roughly a year of listening, first in short bursts of one or two words before moving on to complete phrases. The statistics of two or more languages must be taught to newborns who are bilingual or multilingual. As a result, kids are able to segregate the words they learn into various piles based on variances in the language's rhythmic and pitch patterns (for example: putting into English pile and Spanish pile).

Bilingual children share a single vast map, a library of sounds from all languages, in their brains.

Every language a youngster learns is his or her own. (Meaning KIDS TAKE OWNERSHIP of their new words & phrases and SO SHOULD YOU!)

Needless to say, we can't learn a new language in any kind of womb, but there are important lessons to learn from how babies learn. Even this example is one we can apply to our learning experience.

WHY CAN'T I LEARN THIS?!

The first fact you must know is this: You CAN learn your new language!

However, there are some pretty heavy myths you may have accidentally fallen into.

Myth #1: Children are better at learning a new language than adults.

I just exclaimed how many children are great learners of a new language, but that doesn't make them better than your ability to learn a new language!

But as a matter of fact, there are some people who think the exact opposite. According to developer and blogger Dimitris Gkiokas, who wrote "Why Adults Are Better Learners Than Children," adults are better learners than children (Gkiokas, 2018). While I'm not sure that ruling stands, we can be certain that adult brains can take in new information and grow at any age. In physical condition, there is no reason why an adult can't learn a new language as smoothly as a child. We may have our own set of obstacles (which I'll address later) but don't buy into this myth.

The ability to speak at a high degree of fluency in a foreign language may be achieved by adults in months, while it takes a kid years to reach the same level of fluency. It's just that children find learning languages simpler than adults because of one significant advantage: they're blank slates!

It's our fear of looking stupid that holds us back from diving into the new language. Adults can outperform children in terms of intellect, discipline, and consistency when we set aside our own limitations.

Myth #2: You need to know all that grammar!

You probably have impeccable grammar in your native language. Is it because you carry around conjugation charts in your brain all day long that this happens to you? Is it because you know all the grammatical rules and their formal titles by heart?

No, you picked up your grammar on your own by imitating other people.

No one ever says, "I will having pizza," without everyone around them realizing they said that sentence wrong. However, we'd all understand what the person meant.

Yes, you want to be able to use the grammar of your target language with this kind of ease. This can't be learned through theory.

Grammar theory might actually slow down your learning if you focus in on it too early.

Studying grammar can fuel the flames of perfectionism that our professors have been fanning throughout our educational lives.

Progress is thwarted by the pursuit of perfection.

As a recovering "perfectionist," I can truly feel your pain... This reminds me of my experience while living in New York City. One snowy winter evening, my language teacher and I decided to meet on the corner and head to a study group together after work. It was going to take us a while to walk to Chinatown in this weather, but the reward was well worth it! It had been snowing for quite a while, and as we walked, we noticed the snow had piled up to just over 0.3 m or over a foot high. As we charged along, my language teacher, Steve Epstein (who's a language LEGEND, by the way), said that, unlike other nights, he was only going to talk to me in Chinese until we made it to our destination. As this would push my brain to make new connections and new neural pathways, just like a BABY during the learning process.

At first, it was a different experience, only hearing Steve speak to me in my target language. And after a few minutes, I could feel myself having to work so hard just to scratch and scrape to understand a few sentences… But after I took a deep breath and allowed my brain to relax and soak it in like a sponge, I started to notice a few different patterns! I noticed Steve using this one word over and over in a few different ways. He kept saying the word "Di Fang". So I asked him, as any curious cat would, "What is this word you keep using Di Fang"? And as promised, he said he would answer my question in Chinese and even went on to give me examples of what the word means and how to use it.

The wheels in my brain were turning so hard trying to figure out this all-time mystery, that you could start to see the smoke coming out of my ears. And as the snow continued to land onto our hats, faces, and eyelashes, I was counting the minutes till we would arrive at the study group's door.

But you know, a funny thing happened, in one of those moments out of the movie "A Beautiful Mind" where a few items in your memory start to come into the foreground, light up, and become more crystallized in clarity. I began to notice that my brain had more clearly aligned the grammar, and sentence structure and even connected the other words surrounding the all-mysterious "Di Fang."

Now, after walking up the steps, suddenly arriving at the door of our study group, Steve leans forward to finally reveal the meaning of this now infamous Chinese word "Di Fang" in English. And as I eagerly awaited, seconds feeling like minutes, he plainly said, "It means PLACE." With his snickering grin, like "You silly rabbit". He even kindly goes on to say in English what he was saying on the way there… "You know, like, we're coming from a Di Fang, we're going to a Di Fang, you work at a Di Fang… and so on."

Looking back on that experience, now, as a fluent speaker, I really appreciated the time and patience Steve took with me to allow my brain the opportunity to make those connections their babies and children so often take for granted. As adult language learners, we need to leverage these secret techniques to our advantage and display this level of patience & kindness to ourselves during the process.

In place of correcting, concentrate on establishing a relationship. Does the native speaker talk to you in your own language? Is it possible for you to make your point?

If the answer to this question is yes, then you've achieved your objective. It doesn't matter if you used the wrong preposition -the subtleties will be added afterward.

Myth #3: Learning a second language takes a real special skill.

The fact that I am fluent in many languages has led to the assumption that I have a "natural talent"

for languages. Because of my "special" DNA, they feel that I am capable of learning.

According to folklore, only a few people are born with this particular kind of language-learning DNA. In other words, you must not be a member of this exclusive group of individuals if you are having difficulty learning Spanish.

In light of the reality that any youngster may learn any language from anywhere, this makes no sense at all.

We are all born with the ability to acquire new languages; it's part of what makes us unique as humans.

Because some individuals succeed in learning a foreign language while others do not, why is this the case?

It's as simple as practice and application.

Either you're having trouble putting in enough practice time, or your approach to language learning is flawed. A polyglot's ability to communicate in many languages isn't some kind of natural gift! Rather, it's the result of many hours spent doing the right things over and over again. Most of the abilities we think of as talents are really the result of a lot of hard work and dedication.

At this point, you are fully committed to your native language, so you may have the tendency to translate every single word from the new language to your own. And you probably think this is the best way to learn, right? Wrong! You're putting in some extra work that makes the job so much harder for your brain .

Trust yourself to learn the language "as is."

Here's a **Pro Tip:** DO NOT translate the new language into your own. Just accept the strange sounds of the new language "as they are." (If done correctly, in no time, these sounds will become very familiar, they will not feel strange at all but rather will sound like everyday household words)

DON'T BE AFRAID TO MAKE MISTAKES

Go ahead! Make a few blunders. Take a deep breath and accept the possibility that you'll make blunders.

Don't be afraid to make a lot of errors! The more you rectify your errors, the more fluent you'll become in your new language. This is important to keep in mind since making errors is a necessary part of learning and progressing.

"It's okay to make mistakes sweetheart!" Do you remember when we taught other kids this lesson?

When it comes to learning, mistakes are a necessary part of the process. It's impossible for your brain to learn anything if you don't make errors while you're doing it. It will go on skipping down its merry path, but it will never actually expand. It will never be able to truly learn. So, accept your beautiful blunders, since they are the fuel that powers your growth.

I remember when the leader of my study group, whom we affectionately call Auntie Hattie, asked me to lead the next 5-minute portion of our language lesson the following week. As the words left her mouth, it felt like everyone's heads turned to look at me all at the same time. Uh-oh, now the pressure is on! Auntie Hattie said that I could choose any topic for the next lesson, so I felt a slight relief in that moment. But now I felt pressure to choose an interesting topic that would hold the attention of my classmates.

I was also struggling with feelings of inadequacy, feeling that, essentially I did not know enough yet to teach others.

As the week flew by, I was racking my brain, trying to find a great topic. I asked my friends for suggestions, I scoured through language books and even tried to Google the answer. Suddenly the night before our class, it hit me! I noticed a root word that was present constantly in many sentences throughout our conversations. And the more I examined this word, the more useful it seemed to become. Ah ha, finally, I have it!

The next day, at our study group, my preparation the day before allowed me to feel calm, cool, and collected. There were many other distractions, including a pretty young lady inviting me out for the evening the night before. Thankfully, I had enough strength and fortitude to resist those temptations that would impede my progress to achieving fluency in my target language! As Auntie Hattie invited me up in front of the class, I could feel the curiosity of all the students peak. At the beginning of my presentation, I could even tell that they struggled to see the connection between these root words and how they connect to our everyday speech. I even made a few mistakes in my pronunciation, which drew their attention away from the main point. Fortunately, Auntie Hattie was very reassuring, even mentioning that "no one is perfect. Everybody makes mistakes," and then we quickly moved on. However, as I explained it thoroughly by providing examples and visual aids, I could see the student's eyes light up in excitement! As if they were making new connections in their mind, previously unknown.

Honestly, the five minutes flew by so fast, and I even felt as if I had rediscovered something brand new about this "foreign" language as well myself… which now, is beginning to feel much more comfortable & familiar to me.

Let's look at organizational development writer and motivator Amy McCune's outlook on making mistakes (McCune, 2020). She supports the idea of making mistakes for our personal betterment (in our case, learning a new language).

You may not have realized, but making mistakes is an opportunity to display a lot of leadership skills. Many may see errors as a less-than-perfect human, but that's not true at all. As a matter of fact, our leadership abilities and our character can often be judged through our mistakes. Here are some tips from McCune about the benefits you can find in your own blunders. Let this stay with you as you venture into your language-learning journey.

- Gain new insight.

When we make a mistake, we've been taught that it means we've done something wrong and we've failed. We may obtain insight into what success looks like for ourselves by examining the things that make us feel like we've failed. When we make mistakes, it's a sign that we've lost focus on our goals. For example, if an activity is seen by us as a mistake, it is important to examine why this is the case.

- Face your phobias.

We have a natural apprehension about making errors since adults see them as evil. As a result, we have a tremendous need to protect our egos from being hurt. Recognizing a problem and taking steps to fix it necessitates facing our concerns. The ability to conquer our fears allows us to develop and evolve to the next level. It's a show of strength and resilience to face your fears.

- Demonstrate bravery.

Courage is overcoming one's fear of making errors while speaking and continuing ahead despite the setbacks.

Acknowledging your mistakes and resolving to try something a little different from the norm admittedly requires a lot of guts. Many adults have difficulty figuring out how to be emotionally and psychologically BRAVE when allowing a strange-sounding foreign language to flow freely out of their mouths. Simultaneously the kid standing right next to them, fearlessly walks right up, stares the language in its eye, and literally laughs in its face, making more mistakes than us all, meanwhile these brave little souls are fluently progressing in their language skills each day.

In this aspect, kids teach us a VALUABLE secret lesson... Mistakes allow us adults a chance to display our leadership qualities, and bravery is one of them.

- Encourage originality.

To learn from our mistakes, we must consider other options available to us. They force us to re-examine a problem and develop new ideas or techniques to solve it. When we make mistakes, we learn about what doesn't work, and we're inspired to try new things. Making mistakes are considered learning opportunities in the creative and innovative communities. It is possible to uncover something better if one shifts their attitude in this way.

- Showcase your honesty.

Small errors are typically the precursors to larger ones. Even the tiniest decisions can have an impact, which is why it's critical that we consider the consequences of our daily choices. An error may indicate that our words and actions need to be in sync. Rethinking our goals, objectives, and behaviors is a possible solution in this situation. Our leadership's honesty is on display in how we deal with errors.

- Make a difference by sharing your knowledge.

Many blunders may be used as a teaching tool. Not only does it serve as a lesson for us, but it also offers a chance for us to pass on our knowledge to others. When we are brave enough to share our own challenges with the world, others may be motivated to do the same. As leaders, we may show our team members that it's alright to make errors because we're ready to share our own. This offers us a chance to think about what we might have done differently and how we could have done it better. For leaders, these lessons are essential to pass on.

As mentioned earlier, kids AREN'T AFRAID to make mistakes. That is a learned behavior after childhood.

And since we can't reverse the hands of time and relive our elementary years, let's explore how we can fluently learn to speak a new language just as well (and even better) than a child can!

STOP OVERDOING IT!

At the beginning, getting caught up in the minutiae of learning a new language can be a bit tricky. And sometimes it may feel like you're on a surfboard out in the middle of the ocean, trying to find some point of reference on the horizon. Desperately looking for anything you can relate to. You may be curious about the secrets your target language is hiding and you wish to know why things are the way they are. As a student, we encourage you to go out into the wild and EXPLORE, EXPAND & EXCITE! To quote my good friend Rachel, an expert in her field of Brain-Friendly Grammar & Neuroscience, she says "The brain works better in a curiosity state." And this has been confirmed by the work of Dr. John Ratey, a Clinical Professor at Harvard University (2001). His findings also reveal that "The brain is a pattern-seeking device that relates whole concepts to one another, and looks for similarities, differences or relationships between them." So now using YOUR OWN NATURAL CURIOSITY to explore and uncover the treasures hiding under grammatical structures is actually a secret weapon you can use to propel you forward in making progress to reach your fluency goals. (By the way, this is also one of the hidden techniques that children use all the time to achieve fluency at record speed as well)

So go out into the world, discover, unravel, explore, and make new connections!

Keep in mind that your brain will automatically make use of your native grammatical structures while learning your target language. Research carried out in 2016, indicates that, while learning your target language, running in the background, your brain is taking notice of word order, and if your target language has grammatical properties that are similar to or different from your mother tongue. And research has shown that it helps your brain if you can reuse characteristics from your native language when learning your target language. Also, when your brain cannot make use of existing grammatical structures in your new language, then realizing that it must build up new neural connections to create resources, will help you to be much more patient with yourself during the process.

Being aware that your brain might take a little extra time to strengthen physical connections because it has no existing reference in the brain to connect the new language with, can help you feel much more relaxed and comfortable on your path to fluency.

- Kirsten Weber, Morten H. Christiansen, Karl Magnus Petersson, Peter Indefrey and Peter Hagoort (2016) "fMRI Syntactic and Lexical Repetition Effects Reveal the Initial Stages of Learning a New Language" Journal of Neuroscience 36 (26) 6872-6880

Languages also change in ways that are entirely out of the ordinary.

So balance is also encouraged and also consider the fact that all languages change over time in a variety of ways, and it's vital to remember this. Not every part of language can provide an explanation yet. Sometimes there's just no historical record of why. The gender of words is a common occurrence in many languages, as you're surely aware. In Spanish, a chair is feminine, whereas a stool is masculine. Why is that? You could ask. And I'd be happy to provide you with a clear and accurate explanation. "Because that's the way things are" is, regrettably, the best I can come up with when answering this question. Argh! Surely, there's a purpose behind this?

Right!? In theory, there may be a rationale for everything you learn in etymology, and with enough time & research digging for the answer, we will likely be somewhere in the ballpark of the truth... Maybe...

There are lots of expressions that are completely different from their original meanings.

As a general rule, many people make the error of translating everything word for word, as a beginner. They try to replace each and every word they hear in their mother tongue with what they are learning from their new target language, which at times could be viewed as more transliteration instead of a smooth translation in that sense.

That's why having an EXPERIENCED Translator and learning to become one yourself, is such an INVALUABLE skillset to possess in this modern time of technology, in a world that is ever becoming smaller & more interdependent on each culture and language group working together more closely each year.

It's true that many phrases are indeed completely illogical! And that's OK! That's what languages are all about! In English, there are a lot of strange words and phrases that pop up, so keep that in mind too.

If you're a native English speaker, these idioms may sound natural to you, but they may be entirely foreign to someone who is just beginning to learn the English language. Because you've heard them so often, you're acquainted with a slew of bizarre phrases.

Just remember, it will all work out in the end if you STAY CURIOUS and ask tons of questions! (just like some other little people we know… lol)

Native Speakers don't always say it the way you think they do.

Learning a new language may expose us to a lot of high-quality audio recordings. Because of this, even native speakers might have difficulty following along sometimes. Even while slow and exact pronunciation is necessary for language acquisition, it isn't often how native speakers talk on the street. You may have heard the phrase, "Do you want to travel to Toronto?" while you were studying English. Next, they're approached by someone who asks, "Ya'wanna travel to Trono? ". There's a chance they'll look at you and say, "Wait... What?" "What happened to all these words?" If you're an English speaker, saying "ya'wanna" instead of saying "do you wish to" is entirely normal. However, it's a skill that can only be honed by repetition. Don't be concerned. If you give it time, you'll get the hang of it.

It's important to use grammar to your benefit, yet it's often overused & over-focused on.

Using grammar as a shortcut rather than a hindrance may be quite beneficial while learning a new language. It's critical to remember that grammar is nothing more than a description of the linguistic structure. It's just that simple! Many applications on the market don't teach you any grammar or conjugation and expect you to learn what you need to know via context. That's a blunder, in our opinion. Preparation is key. By studying grammar principles prior to immersion in a new language, you will reinforce the rules rather than struggle to understand them.

When it comes to grammar, overuse is a common concern. There is a short explanation for practically every rule of grammar, and then there is the really lengthy explanation. It takes just a few minutes to grasp the gist of the rule. For the time being, don't strive to grasp all the nuances at the beginning.

Take a look at a few instances and then continue on to learning the grammatical rules. Permit your innate proclivity for language acquisition to take control. In most circumstances, exposure to your new language will resolve any issues that may arise.

While learning a new language, it's simple to give oneself a migraine. Take a break from anything you're working on and come back to it later. Now take a deep breath, Ahhhhh... Everything will fall into place in due course. First, you need to incorporate the new language into your everyday life in a variety of ways. Relax and take in the scenery by watching movies, listening to music, reading, and SPEAKING as much as possible. Your language-learning journey will benefit significantly from this. I recommend this technique if you're looking for an easy-to-understand method of studying genuine grammar, and conjugation.

Research shows a child can learn up to 6 -7 languages simultaneously. Studies also show how the brain must create a new physical space when learning a new foreign language and how that space is best used when the person inputs or learns multiple languages at the same time, to fill that space in the brain.

Just as when a heavy-duty commercial truck creates space in the cargo area to carry a heavy load. But what if the workers only load ONE box onto the truck, shut the doors and send it off? When the truck takes off to its destination, what happens? You will notice that the box tumbles all around the cargo area, the truck does not drive as well behind the wheel, and the engine is not as efficient. However, when the workers load the truck properly, with a FULL or MEDIUM SIZE load, what happens? You will notice that the boxes are safe & secure, the truck drives and handles the road better, and the engine is more efficient.

It's the same inside your brain!

Your brain works better, and it makes learning EASIER when you learn multiple languages at the same time.

Imagine you're observing a group of kids growing up in a multi-lingual environment. It's fascinating how effortlessly they seem to pick up different languages, right? Well, researchers like Dr. François Grosjean have actually studied this phenomenon. They found that when kids are exposed to multiple languages from a young age, their brains just soak it all in like a sponge. It's as if their brains are hard-wired to handle learning multiple languages all at once!

Now, let's dive into the science behind it. Dr. Laura-Ann Petitto and her team at the University of Washington have been exploring how the brain processes languages. Using fancy brain imaging techniques, like functional magnetic resonance imaging (fMRI), they discovered that bilingual brains look different from those of people who only speak one language. Those of us who are working hard to become bilingual have brains that actually exhibit structural and functional differences compared to monolinguals, indicating that the brain undergoes plastic changes in response to language experience. It's like bilingual brains have this special ability to juggle multiple languages seamlessly without breaking a sweat. (Petitto et al., 2012)

But here's the really cool part: learning multiple languages doesn't just make you fluent in languages—it also gives your brain a work-out! Dr. Ellen Bialystok and her colleagues at York University found that bilingual folks have better problem-solving skills and sharper cognitive abilities. It's like becoming bilingual is like going to the gym for your brain!

Other research, such as that by Patricia K. Kuhl and Michael T. Ullman, also explores how neural plasticity and cognitive factors influence language learning across each person's lifespan, hinting at the possibility of varying degrees of language learning aptitude at different ages during your life.

So, bottom line: YOU CAN TOTALLY LEARN MULTIPLE LANGUAGES all at once. And our brains are hard-wired to handle it. Plus, learning more than one language is like giving your brain a SUPERPOWER BOOST. It's pretty amazing what our brains are capable of, don't you think?

***Language Advice from Professional Language Coaches for our readers and learners:**

(Here are a few **Pro Tips** to remember, that really helped me to fluently become MULTILINGUAL)

"Do not translate in your head... Actually **THINK in the language!**"

That means, instead of thinking, "Oh! I just heard this person say "La Mesa" in Spanish next to me... Hmmm, what does that mean again? Uhmm... Oh, I remember.

Instead, you want to replace that type of thinking, by Learning Languages Just Like a Kiddo! Remember, a baby doesn't translate while acquiring language, they just absorb the language "As-Is". They say to themselves, "Hmmm... I just heard this person say "La Mesa", and I see them put dinner & drinks on La Mesa, I can see La Mesa is the thing we do homework on and place food on top of, we all sit around La Mesa together when we eat, and it is just next to the kitchen." Cha' Ching! La Mesa means "Table."

Congratulations! Your language has now been acquired! Babies actually THINK in the target language, in order to actually acquire their language at lightning-fast speeds.

AVOID getting stuck on grammar "from a book" while trying to acquire your target language.

Remember, babies don't study grammar from a book, they **learn by actually speaking the language OUT LOUD.**

Get moving while learning your new language!

Yes, that means you want to actually get up and **MOVE YOUR BODY while learning.**

Have you ever stopped to notice the only time children stop moving during the day?

Most adults would probably say, "When they are sleeping"… LOL… "When they're eating" (eeehhhh… sometimes)… or "Maybe when they are watching cartoons." And that's exactly the point!… The rest of their waking hours during the day kids are in constant motion. (Hillman 2008)(Chen 2013)(Glenberg 2012)

That is another secret to their success in becoming FEARLESSLY FLUENT FAST.

When I look back on my own language-learning journey as an adult, I must say that I have also used this secret weapon to become fluent over and over again. You see, using the part of your brain called the motor cortex to drive the language-learning process in the background is like giving Popeye a full can of power spinach, boosting your ability to think, improving your cognitive performance, memory, vocabulary recall, vocabulary retention, grammar comprehension, overall language proficiency and information processing, all of which are essential for language learning.

Another reason children acquire multiple languages at the same time is due to their miraculous ability to just **throw fear out the window** and not care at all how other people view them or their intelligence. Which leads kids to **ASK QUESTIONS about everything** under the sun. So don't be afraid to 'bug the crap out of people' around you! (Just like kids)

Your future "fluent self" will thank you!

- Hillman, C. H., Erickson, K. I., & Kramer, A. F. (2008). Be smart, exercise your heart: exercise effects on brain and cognition. Nature Reviews Neuroscience, 9(1), 58-65.
- Chen, Z., Lei, Y., Ding, J., & Peng, D. (2013). Moving to learn: The effects of body movements on vocabulary learning. British Journal of Educational Technology, 44(5), E149-E152.
- Glenberg, A. M., & Gallese, V. (2012). Action-based language: A theory of language acquisition, comprehension, and production. Cortex, 48(7), 905-922.
- Bialystok, E. (2017). The bilingual adaptation: How minds accommodate experience. Psychological Bulletin, 143(3), 233–262.
- Grosjean, F. (2010). Bilingual: Life and Reality. Harvard University Press.
- Petitto, L. A., et al. (2012). The "Perceptual Wedge Hypothesis" as the basis for bilingual babies' phonetic processing advantage: New insights from fNIRS brain imaging. Brain and Language, 121(2), 130–143.
- Michael T. Ullman, "A neurocognitive perspective on language: The declarative/procedural model," 2001
- Patricia K. Kuhl, "Early language acquisition: Cracking the speech code," 2004.

CHAPTER 2

USE MEMORY HOOKS

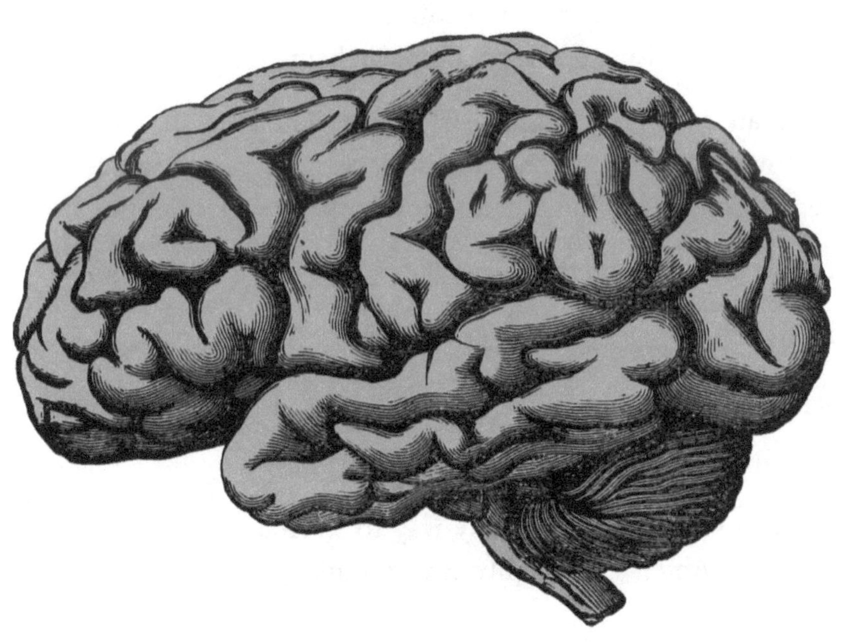

 *"The true art of memory is the art of attention."*

— SAMUEL JOHNSON

We know about using memory, but what does a "hook" have anything to do with this?

Hooking is one of the few memory 'tricks' you can play to recall the meaning of words. There's a "hook" is the word you are trying to recall, which means there's something, like an image, that can make you suddenly remember what the word means (Warren, 2021). To put it another way, you look for hints of what the word means in the foreign word itself. You'll end up "hooking" to the word visually or audibly, depending on how it sounds. There are times when a hook is not immediately apparent, but it is possible that a story or visual representation can help.

Here's an example: In Spanish, 'ojo means 'eyes'. If you know anything about emojis and all the faces that can be made with letters through text, this word almost looks like a face.

Refer to the image on the right.

The two o's are eyes and the 'j' is the nose!

Do you see it now?

It's hard to unsee it once you do catch on.

This may seem like a very silly way to learn a new language, but this works. And it's not as silly as you think.

DO I REALLY NEED TO DO MEMORY TRICKS?

Throughout the day, we all use a number of memory tactics to help us keep a firm hold on the many pieces of information, learn & retain abstract concepts, and even remember different people's faces we encounter in our day-to-day. You have no idea how much you are already doing this. Your mind is plugging in visuals to recall information all day long. According to Regina Richards, writer for Reading Rockets, people use memory tactics like hooking all the time (Richards, 2009).

So ask yourself how you recall something:

Do you recite a phone number aloud to yourself a few times to be sure you remember it?

Do you hold up four fingers to remind yourself to remember four things when you arrive at the grocery store and want to recall four items?

It's difficult for many of us to recall a wedding we attended a few years ago. Food may be the first thing that comes to mind for some. Many of us may remember the bride's gown. Others may be able to recollect the style of the room. Once you've got a hold of the recollection, every time you think about it, more details pop into your head.

Is there anything you do while you're driving home that helps you recall an important phone call?

Dogs bark, and your kids have important things to tell you, as soon as you walk in the door. You're out of paper to jot down a quick note. The chant "call so-and-so," or something similar, may be sung or chanted by a few individuals. The action of walking into the den to lay down their gift may trigger a memory to make the phone call for those who envision a connection.

Throughout the day, we use a range of techniques to help us recall the many information and concepts that we need to keep. The usage of strategies is a vital component of our educational process. These methods aid in the organization and retention of data, as well as the development of a purposeful learning process. Our minds are selective. Patterns in information are more likely to be remembered by the brain.

KNOW HOW YOUR OWN BRAIN WORKS!

If you're going to master this new language thing, you need your brain to work for you. That means you need to know how your brain works in the first place.

So many people give up on learning their foreign language because they just don't know HOW to approach studying a foreign language. It's as if they forgot to update their operating system first, before moving forward to load all their language apps onto their mobile device.

(I mean, as adults, we mostly just forgot how to approach a strange language since it was so long ago that we were children… This fact alone can be a HUGE comfort to you & provide you with SUPERHUMAN confidence, YES you can strike your superhero pose now, knowing that you have already succeeded at this foreign language thing before. That's right, you have something babies don't have, this most valuable possession under your belt called EXPERIENCE… After all, babies don't pop out of their mother's womb fluently speaking their native language, do they?)

Some people think it's about vocab drills or mindless repetition. While going over and reviewing new words isn't wrong, it's just not entirely that efficient. Using memory hooks, and other ways to associate these new words to your world around you is making your amazing brain work for you.

Memory is a multi-step process that requires the cooperation of many different parts. It's merely a representation of what we've learned since our brains really process information in an integrated manner.

Everything starts as a response to the stimuli we get from the world around us. Using our senses, we are able to detect and respond to a variety of stimuli. Our brains have a system for removing and discarding information that isn't relevant or important, like the texture of the carpet under our feet or the sound of the air conditioner. Relevant data is organized into meaningful patterns using the same filtering method.

Short-term memory is where information that has been "grabbed" or made meaningful is stored.

When something is out of the ordinary, our brains are trained to pay attention to it. Novelty, whether in the form of comedy, movement, or music, aids in capturing our attention.

Strategies play a crucial role when it comes to organizing information so that it may be stored in long-term memory in a manner that is meaningful and remembered. We need to keep new information from being "dumped" in order to build a long-lasting memory. As a result, we can link it to other pieces of information that already exist.

To be permanently remembered in long-term memory, relevant information must first be encoded in another portion of the brain. Long-term memory can be represented by a file cabinet. Instead of storing the full memory as a single file, the various parts of the experience are kept in separate folders within the file cabinet.

Each person has a unique manner of processing and retaining information when considering how memory works. A memory may be stored in a variety of ways, just as there are many ways to arrive at a particular destination. Route A and Route B are two different ways to get to the grocery store. Either way works. While one individual may like to recall a list by singing it, another person may prefer to envision the items on their list within a "Mind Palace", and so on and so forth. There is no single right way.

Your brain works together and fluidly works within your new language, kind of like Bruce Lee's philosophy on Kung Fu in the book "The Art of Expressing The Human Body".

He says "Using NO WAY as way & having NO LIMIT as limitation."

Spoken like a true Multi-Lingual Master.

MANY WAYS TO HOOK

There are quite a few ways to use hooks for learning a language.

Esther Heerema, a licensed social worker helping patients with dementia, has some wise words. Initially, you can choose a term that evokes an association with the foreign word. In order to learn a new word, you begin by imagining a picture or term associated with that word's meaning.

- The Keyword

Imagine a gate with a cat perched on top of it before you begin learning the Spanish word for cat,

"gato," which when translated means "cat." When it comes to their beginnings, the "a" sound in gato is shorter than the "a" sound in gate. As a result, the proper term should be remembered as a result of seeing and associating with it.

- Chunking Phrases

Chunking is a memorization technique that breaks down a large amount of information into smaller chunks that are easier to remember, such as phrases, words, or even numbers. There is a good chance that remembering the following number: 3108675309 will be a challenge. As a result, 310 867 5309 is easier to recall when chunked like this. I mean, think about it, this "Chunking-Down" technique works so well, song writers even used it to make millions of dollars with a #1 hit song on the radio using that same combination of numbers you just memorized!

People with moderate Alzheimer's disease can benefit from chunking-down, as a more brain-friendly language acquisition approach. (Heerema, 2015) It's worth pondering. Techniques like this one have helped patients with mental illnesses who struggle to remember information. Learning a new language can definitely be achievable if it's demonstrated to aid and improve verbal working memory in the early stages of dementia.

- Get Your Groove On!

Using music as a means of encoding information into your brain has also been shown to be very effective for acquiring your new language. You can learn so much more when it's put to music, like the "A-B-C" song, which is a classic example. All of these things and more are available to you here in this program included later in the book.

In order to explore the amazing potential of this concept further, you can use pre-existing songs, which you may find on the internet, or can choose to compose completely new songs of your own. Something pretty interesting happens when you create your own song. Not only can you recite the song by heart, which may be very short & sweet. But something a bit less obvious is taking place deep within you behind the scenes. You secretly tell your brain that it's now okay to take ownership of your new language and that it is now YOURS. You don't even have to be able to sing or write music properly to use this mnemonic strategy and remember it.

- Words and Letters

Acronyms and acrostics are among the most common methods of memorizing information. This basic formula of a letter represents each word or phrase that has to be memorized by the acronym.

As an example, think of the National Basketball Association, which stands for the NBA. Unlike an acronym, an acrostic develops a phrase that aids in memory rather than a new "word" that is formed.

A common acrostic in the classroom is: "Please Excuse My Dear Aunt Sally". This acrostic mnemonic illustrates the algebraic sequence of operations and stands for Parentheses, Exponents, Multiplication & Division, Addition & Subtraction.

- It's Rhyme Time!

"Oh Mary Mack, Mack, Mack. All dressed in black, black, black. With silver buttons, buttons, buttons, all down her back, back, back..." Is there anything further you can add to this nursery rhyme?

Repetition and rhyming are often factors in children's ability to recall and learn nursery rhymes. Is it possible to employ rhyming terms to aid in your memory and recall newly learned knowledge?

Words may be made to rhyme by rearranging them or by using a different word with the same meaning.

Take the well-known rule of "i" before "e," except after "c" or in words that sound like "ay," such as "neighbor" or "weigh." We remember this statement not just because we've heard it so many times but also because of the rhymes that it contains.

- Make a Connection

You may use mnemonic strategies to help you remember new knowledge by relating it to something you already know. As a result, it gains significance and becomes simpler to recall. Elaborative rehearsal may be used for nearly any topic or kind of material by making connections.

Think of Jeffery as an example of a person you've just met. Pay attention to how you can recall his name instead of rushing through it. If you've ever seen Jeffery be very animated, you may draw the logical conclusion that Jeffery is synonymous with bouncing about in his work. When you see him again, you will suddenly see 'Jumping Jeffery,' you'll be able to say, "Hello by name." When you meet him, just don't include the term "jumping" in his name.

- Putting the Pieces in Place

Storytelling, building a Mind Palace or creating a visual representation of what you need to remember will help you recall what you've learned. You're reminded of the following thing when you recollect the last.

When you have to carry your homework papers, glasses, gym shoes, wallet, lunch money, and keys to school in the morning, you'll need some type of checklist or Excel Spreadsheet to keep track of everything you need to bring.

The following short narrative could be used to illustrate the linking system: Putting on their spectacles and workout shoes, Jack's homework papers rushed into his wallet, where his ravenous keys were chomping down on his lunch money. These are some great examples of using a few hooks to improve your memory.

YOUR GOLDEN TICKET TO BECOMING THE LINGUISTIC LIFEGUARD OF TOMORROW

"Learning a language is like making pasta. You gotta let it simmer, taste occasionally, and throw some noodles at the wall to see what sticks."

— LINGUINI LANG, PASTA LINGUIST

Hey there, Language Rockstar! Remember when we dove headfirst into the linguapool at the start of this book? We chatted about how every language learner, from baby babblers to eloquent orators, has a tale to tell... That golden nugget was what sparked this whole book venture.

You see, life's mishaps aren't just for blooper reels. We evolve by goofing up sometimes, by eavesdropping on foreign convos (all in the name of learning, promise!), by parroting catchy song lyrics, and by swapping our funniest linguistic slip-ups.

This, right here, is where YOU get to jump on the proverbial language bandwagon. Think of all those polyglot celebrities, like Bradley Cooper, who casually flips between English and French in interviews, or Mila Kunis, who can sass you up in both English and Russian. They take their linguistic prowess and inspire many to pick up a language or two.

While you might not have shared screen time with Rocket the Raccoon or Meg Griffin, you, dear reader, have a power move up your sleeve: to boost OTHER language enthusiasts' confidence!

By blessing this book with your review on Amazon, Apple Books (or whichever platform you prefer), you'll light up the path for others in search of the linguistic Holy Grail. By spilling the tea on how this book leveled-up your language game, you're basically handing out free language compasses.

Thank you from the bottom of my multilingual heart!

Now you've got some linguistic mountains to conquer ahead, but with your map-sharing spirit, YOU'RE already A BEACON OF HOPE for others. Sharing our arduous and wonderful language journeys together ensures that the global game of "Telephone" keeps on progressing FLUENTLY.

***"By leaving a review of this book on Amazon" Click HERE , or* Scan the QR code below**

Cheers to you, the soon-to-be linguistic legend!

CHAPTER 3
SAY IT LOUD...!

 *"Language is a living thing. We can feel it changing. Parts of it become old: they drop off and are forgotten. New pieces bud out, spread into leaves, and become big branches, proliferating."*

— GILBERT HIGHET

There are many skills in language learning… However, the four main skills that people generally tend to focus on are: listening, speaking, reading, and writing. Practicing all four aspects on a regular basis can help you learn more effectively since they are interconnected.

It's common for individuals to focus more on some abilities than others. Surprisingly, the majority of individuals want to excel at speaking. Despite this, it's the one they work on the least.

It's not enough to just know; we must open our mouths and put it into practice. It isn't enough to just be willing; we must also act. If it seems too philosophical, well that's really rather accurate! People may not practice speaking out loud as often as they should since they may feel it's inconvenient for them at the moment. When it comes to communicating, you need to interact with other people. Having a discussion in our native language is something we do instinctively as human beings. Conversations, on the other hand, are very difficult for computers to master. Even if a computer can solve the most difficult equations, recall enormous amounts of information, and beat the best chess players in the world, it will never be able to have a meaningful discussion with you. Even if you've got a virtual assistant on your phone, it's probably not going to be that funny. You must converse with actual people in order to improve your communication abilities (scary, I know). Computers may not be able to have a meaningful conversation with you, but they can help you locate the amazing people who are essential to your progress.

Having a solid grounding in your new language before venturing out into the world might be beneficial, but do not procrastinate too long! When traveling to other countries, we recommend that you attempt to communicate in the local language as soon as you begin learning the language, even if you just know a few phrases like "hello" and "thank you." As a result, you'll be more equipped to deal with future bouts of language phobia. When you make an effort to learn a new language, you'll be surprised at how much other people appreciate it. Keep in mind that there will never be an ideal time to begin talking. Isn't it better to get started as soon as possible? Most individuals have difficulty communicating because THEY DON'T TALK OFTEN ENOUGH. I realize this is a no-brainer, but despite the obviousness, many adults have trouble grasping the concept of language. While theory is important, it's only as good as what you do with it that matters. Just ask any kid on the playground. Even the shy children, who are quiet by nature, can be heard using the new phrases they just picked up from their friends.

Getting started on the piano without ever picking up a keyboard is a unique and unusual path to follow. But do you think that it would work? A hands-on method, on the other hand, would be completely meaningless if you had never heard of a piano before. The most important thing is to receive a lot of exposure to the sounds, but also a lot of hands-on work is equally important. What am I trying to get at here? Hands-on practice (also known as speaking... Lol) is sometimes overlooked when it comes to learning a new language. We all learn a foreign language in school, but most of us never USE what we've learned outside of the classroom. It's unfortunate that grade school language programs aren't meant to help students communicate but rather to help them pass their tests. We tend to forget a lot of what we've learned in school because we never put it to work.

When learning a new language, many individuals experience some degree of anxiety. Fortunately, after only a few discussions, the feeling of wanting to be flawless is usually banished from our minds into the deep dark abyss for good. Even if it takes you a while to find the right words, you'll come to realize that you have nothing to be afraid of. It's so satisfying to finally be able to communicate and express your feelings in a foreign language, and it's likely what you're looking for out of any program you purchase. After having finished a discussion in a foreign language, you'll feel so accomplished that it's impossible to describe. It would be a pity to deprive yourself of that pleasure for so long. We strongly advise you to begin speaking out loud as soon as you are comfortable doing so.

Then, you could ask, "Good advice wise guy, but how am I expected to do that?" There is no better time to meet new people than NOW, as technology has made it simpler than ever before to interact with others. Learning a language does not need a two-year stint on a coffee plantation in some faraway country. In fact, in the following sections, we'll be going through all the many ways you may use your new language on a regular basis to improve your communication skills.

SPEAK IT EVERYWHERE!

Because we've been out of practice for so long, it may be difficult to put this new language to good use in every scenario we find ourselves in, and it can take a little bit more effort for some of us to reach a level of mastery. In the minds of many, the ultimate objective is to speak their language and to be understood by other native speakers. And yet, they seldom ever put any effort into honing their audible communication skills. I would love to shout this from the rooftops! As soon as possible, you should include speaking into your study regimen!

Dialogue isn't always necessary. When listening to a new language, you might begin by repeating the words aloud to improve your pronunciation. Using your target language, you can even talk to yourself. Be sure to talk to yourself in that language whenever possible, and make it a habit to do so. It has the potential to work miracles, and it's quite easy to use. You often see children doing it. And let me tell you, your brain will thank you later.

I have used this method to improve my fluency for years now, and it has done wonders for helping other people to understand me better. It also has helped me to discover what specific things to do that have ensured I pronounced my words clearly.

If you have the chance to use the language in the real world, that's the best way to learn how to do it.

However, even if no one else is nearby, you have a wealth of resources at your disposal. The internet is all you need to get started. Even free language learning programs like Pimsleur Language, Fluent U, Duolingo, and language-exchange programs like italki.com can help you learn a new language at a reasonable price. Speaking a foreign language for the first time may be a frightening experience, but once you get the rhythm of the language, the rewards are immeasurable.

But are you relying only on grammatical rules and written exercises to learn a new language?

Is your attention focused on the language's tiniest details?

Doing a slew of word-by-word translations again?

Indeed, mastering the three skills of reading, writing, and listening is critical to success. However, you won't go very far if you don't build fluency in speaking, which is an essential component.

Students who concentrate on rules and correct writing but do not practice their speech out loud often struggle to comprehend native speakers and choke in real-life interactions. That's not something we want you to experience.

In order to make new acquaintances and impress others, I want you to behave like a native while conversing with a native. The more you speak your target language out loud, the better you'll be able to learn, remember it and speak it fluently. The greatest aspect is that you may use this method over & over again to learn any language you desire.

Let's look at ways to speak out loud as much as you can. And for those moments you can't (because not everybody is learning your language), there's an answer for that too!

When you're reading or writing, say the words out loud in an undertone to yourself.

Writing is also an essential component of learning a new language, so don't ignore it. Exercises that test your knowledge in a variety of areas, including answering questions, selecting the proper word for a phrase, writing a few paragraphs of text and emails are required for you to grow as well.

Almost all grammar textbooks include a part for review and practice exercises. The most efficient way to solve these portions is to read them out loud rather than mechanically.

You should read aloud or write in your target language whenever possible.

While doing this, don't be scared to be funny and attempt to replicate a real native's accent. This mastery of syntax and vocabulary will show via good speaking once you enter into a discussion.

You'll also get a sense of self-assurance, which is essential for advancement.

- Think-it when you can't say it!

You're not considered proficient in another language unless you find yourself thinking in that language on a regular basis. That's a good point. If you happen to find yourself continuously thinking in your native language and doing mental translations, you'll never be able to reach high levels of fluency.

Please allow me to save you precious time & painful frustration.

Think in the target language as much as possible at the beginning of your practice. This method will propel you forward. Your most frequently used words and phrases should be learned FIRST in your target tongue.

Translate all the short and easy statements you use in your everyday conversations into the target language you're currently studying. Then, when you go shopping, think of what you normally bring with you... What items do you normally pick up at the market?... Where are you traveling from?... From the park? Or maybe from the gym?... What mode of transportation are you using? Are you headed to the office? Or hmmm, let me guess, you just might be at home laid back all comfy on the couch, aren't you? Remember, as you go about your everyday routine, you can repeat these short phrases in your head.

Using a literal translation isn't always the best option for you. You'll have to conduct a little research to find out how various phrases are used in the language you're learning since idioms often demand a lot of latitude in interpretation. An excellent way to recall conversational idioms is to PRACTICE SAYING THEM OUT LOUD.

- Imitate What You Hear.

Do you recall that swoon-worthy romantic film you saw in French? It's worth a second look! Because this is a great learning approach, you won't become bored even when you've seen the characters before. Take numerous pauses in between and make sure to mimic the dialogue with the same pitch, pace & power as you heard it spoken.

Take a look at the actors' accents as well and mimic them!

Take time to notice their breathing pattern as they speak.

And make sure to have fun!

Try to mimic what the characters are saying ASAP. You'll notice just as soon as you're able to move your tongue more quickly, something amazing begins to happen, you will start to notice yourself juggle those unfamiliar sounds more effortlessly! You will sound just like a native! And suddenly the foreign language isn't so foreign to you anymore. It is starting to become part of who you are. The strange sounds suddenly begin to feel more normal and commonplace, everyday, and natural. This method also helps you to retain and recite HOW native speakers say things in the heat of the moment. Impersonating a real person also means that your accent will come to resemble that of the native speakers you're imitating over time.

- Learn the words of songs & music in your foreign language by listening to them regularly.

When you sing, the words come out effortlessly, and you can typically pronounce them more correctly.

As a bonus, listening to music helps you immerse yourself in the culture you're studying. If you want to improve your fluency, you must, of course, listen to music with lyrics. Sing along with the song, if the words to your song are available to look up. Lyrics for almost any song, in any language, even every dialect, may be found thanks to the Internet's vast repository of knowledge (if necessary).

Please keep in mind that nobody really cares whether you're a good musician or not. The only thing that matters is that you stay in sync with the rhythm of the speech. Singing connects the words to your brain's memory bank in a way that no other method can.

- Read it aloud.

A great writer may be found in every society or nation. In Spanish, we have Miguel de Cervantes. In Chinese, we have Li Bai. In French, we have Hugo, and in Russian, we have the great Tolstoy and Dostoevsky. It's critical to immerse yourself in the language's literary canon. When you read it aloud, it's much more enjoyable. As an additional option, try your luck at several online literary assessments.

Poetry has an even more significant impact since it teaches you about meter and cadence. It goes without saying that poetry requires a greater degree of fluency to be fully appreciated.

- Talk to a native speaker.

You saw this one coming, didn't you?

Being able to impress native speakers with your knowledge of vocabulary and pronunciation is an indication that you are a competent speaker of the language. Learning a new language with a group of friends may be a tremendous source of encouragement, but they can't replace the need for native speakers.

If you're going to a new nation to learn a new language, you may want to consider bringing a friend along. Ask around to see if anybody is ready to assist you. Although you'll have to show them tremendous respect for their time, this might lead to a beautiful relationship! You may also want to consider spending a semester abroad if you're planning on attending college (and have an established budget). Language and cultural institutions in certain nations, like Germany, provide a broad variety of programs. There is always the Internet to fall back on if that fails.

- Analyze the variety of the language.

Now that you've mastered the conventional version of the language, it's time to tackle the more challenging material of mastering different dialects. First, you could start by learning about the numerous dialects spoken by indigenous people in other regions of your nation, and The First Nations in your region. For example, in the United States, there are large differences in pronunciation between the East Coast, West Coast, and Southern regions. Try to study vocabulary words that are distinctive to a variety of regions and experiment with how the same phrases are pronounced throughout North America & Europe.

It will not take you a lifetime to master a foreign language. Please keep in mind that nothing in this world is beyond your reach.

You'll always be able to achieve new heights!

Having fun is a major characteristic shared by all of the approaches outlined in our boutique service we provide learners in our program. We are passionate about helping

NATIVE ENGLISH SPEAKERS from around the world find SUCCESS on their journey to FLUENCY.

*Pro Tip:** Just like children practice, as an adult make sure to find ways to have FUN at each step, while learning your new language.

These neuroscientific approaches are elegantly designed, time tested and proven ways to assist you in improving your fluency, without causing you any major disruptions to your current lifestyle!

BUG THE MESS OUT OF PEOPLE!

 *"What makes us human, I think, is an ability to ask questions, a consequence of our sophisticated spoken language."*

— JANE GOODALL

Obviously, you're not out to drive anybody crazy. However, as I've mentioned before, this is a must read, and has truly proven to be a technique that has helped me become fluent multiple times over, at several different stages of my life. Plus it's used by children every day: Go out to actually talk to the native speakers! This should be a top goal for you. For some people maybe a scary goal, but a HUGELY IMPORTANT GOAL nonetheless.

Well, actually, it's not fair to say scary. Just more like taking a significant level of commitment on your part.

You know that fright you feel that only springs from the idea of "messing up." That is what many people may experience when approaching a native speaker to practice for the first time. But you have no idea how much people appreciate you wanting to learn their language!

And let's be real: In everyday life, real circumstances will pop up, especially experiences in which you are compelled to speak a foreign language with others, and these very experiences just may provide some of the finest opportunities for true growth that you will come across on your path to fluency. And 99% of the time, you can reach down and pick up these "Golden Nuggets" of opportunity in your very own city.

Sometimes bugging the mess out of your friends, family, and even strangers is not easy. But boy, is it worth it! There are some moments in your journey to becoming fluent that define you and shape you as a student. These were some of the "Ah Ha!" moments that really made me feel like a kid again!... It was a lovely spring day, walking down the busy streets of Chinatown. As my language teacher and I walked side-by-side, all of the street signs and advertisements started to catch my eye.

Just like a kid, I started to ask my language teacher, Steve, "What does this sign mean? Oooo... And what about that one over there?"... Really just bugging the mess out of him as we walked along. Then, I started to recognize a few words in my target language on another sign posted on a building... But before Steve could finish answering my question, I immediately asked, "What about that one? What does that sign mean?"

After listening to his explanation, I found a sign that I could actually read! I elbowed Steve on the shoulder repeatedly, shouting, "I know that one, I know that one!" I knew all the words, pictures & symbols on the sign! I could actually read the whole sign! I couldn't believe it! I was actually reading my new foreign language spontaneously, on the street, 'in the wild' with native speakers! I was like a kid in a candy store!

I could see the look on Steve's face. And oh boy... I knew I was bugging the mess out of him. I just couldn't help it though. I was full-on. He was a bit frustrated, but even he found it hard to be too upset with me because I was so excited! After a while Steve's face also reflected the feelings of warmth and that he was proud of me, probably because I was actually using all the things that he had worked so hard to help me acquire. He could see the joy radiating from me all over my face.

I felt so powerful. I felt vindicated. Finally, all of my hard work was paying off! I was honestly walking on sunshine as we moved down the street. And I appreciate Steve soooo much for being extremely patient with me. He even took extra time to point out other Chinese characters on the buildings that we had previously learned during our lessons with the study group. Little did I know, my brain had been soaking up all these different words along the way like a sponge the whole time.

Thank God, at that moment, I was such a kid at heart! And thank Steve for letting me bug the mess out of him on so many occasions! Haha.

When it comes to gaining real-world experience, traveling or studying abroad is the most convenient option. You'll have the chance to interact with native speakers of the language you wish to learn, as well as other learners who don't speak your original tongue.

Organizations like the Peace Corps often use this strategy to send volunteers with little or no prior knowledge of a foreign language to completely new environments. However, despite the discomfort, these circumstances are a great motivator to learn rapidly.

If your circumstances don't allow you to go somewhere physically, you may still gain a lot of experience speaking a foreign language by immersing yourself in everyday settings that allow you to use your language naturally. Try the following:

- Weekly or bimonthly language sessions would be perfect. Just find your comfort level. You may either pay your language partner or offer to swap an hour of practice speaking their language for an hour of practice in the language you'd like to study together.
- Join a discussion group! Put your Google-searching skills to the best use by looking up local groups. Students of a foreign language might routinely gather in conversation clubs in their towns and schools to develop their communication skills in an informal setting.
- Consider using an online tutoring or language exchange service. This is a better option for online engagement because you're actually talking to someone rather than reading words off a website. Preply.com and My Language Exchange can help you meet individuals who speak the language you wish to learn. Chatting online with native speakers may help you improve your language skills even if you don't meet them in person.
- Get to know the local immigrants speaking your desired language in your area. Look for volunteer opportunities on sites like VolunteerMatch or Idealist or directly contact groups that support immigrants who speak the language you wish to learn by contacting them personally. You'll never know what you may learn. A whole cultural experience may be waiting just for you!
- **Pro Tip:** Visit places in your city where the majority of the customers speak the language you're trying to learn. Whether it's a Mexican restaurant, or a grocery store

catering to the local Chinese population, you can practice your language skills with the staff, customers and owners of these establishments.

TAP INTO THE CULTURE

I've mentioned getting to know the local immigrants in your area. Knowing more about the people of the language enriches your learning experience so much deeper than you would ever think.

In order to really learn a new language, one must go beyond just memorizing vocabulary and grammar. If you know how to pronounce "lemon" and "glass" in French, it doesn't guarantee you can purchase lemonade at a Parisian coffee shop. In fact, you may be astonished by what you get!

When trying to communicate with a native speaker, you need to do more than just look up words in a dictionary. You need context and an understanding of how to connect the new words you're learning. Because of this, it is impossible to acquire a language independent of its cultural context.

This is one reason why kids learn new languages so fast! Think about how much fun kids have with language while on their local playground. Listen to how children speak when they are having fun. Knowing this secret, now you can learn your next foreign language FAST too!

As you learn a new language, it's also important to understand the cultural context in which it's being used. It's so much simpler to acquire new words, idioms, and manners of speaking when you have a solid understanding of the social context.

To be able to converse with native speakers, one must have a firm grasp of the culture in question. In our modern day, most colleges and even high schools fund exchange programs to provide students with the opportunity to study abroad in a foreign country.

Learning a language is more fun when it is infused with a sense of cultural identity.

When learning a new language, it is crucial to have a strong desire to learn the verbs, tenses, adverbs, phrasal verbs, and so on. After the first three classes, some might feel overwhelmed since you'll be learning hundreds of new words and maybe even a few unknown letters of the alphabet.

Putting all this new knowledge into a cultural context will help you interact with the foreign language on a deeper level. Learning about the lives and habits of native speakers keeps you engaged in the process of learning a new language.

To really grasp a culture, one must go beyond the pages of a dictionary or a textbook. In order to learn more about the people in the area, you may utilize a variety of sources:

- Movies! Students who watched English movies improved their hearing and speaking abilities more quickly than those who did not. Subtitled rather than dubbed films and TV shows might offer you a more authentic picture of how native speakers talk. You'll begin to pick up on cultural cues like specific expressions, accents, and vocal timbres as you continue to practice the language you're learning. We'll talk further about this later in the book.
- Newspapers and magazines. What you study in school and what you read in magazines are two completely different things. As a result, columns reflect how individuals converse with one another in real life. They adhere to all grammatical guidelines while maintaining a conversational tone.

- Use social media! They may help you learn the language of the place you're visiting. Improve your vocabulary and learn words that are only found in the "urban" dictionary if you're in a certain niche.

Learning a language via reading creative works of fiction is both a motivation and a strategy. You can observe how the author has constructed phrases and what new meanings they offer to certain words by reading the passage.

In order to increase your language abilities, travel is the best way to do so. You'll be able to converse with the locals as well as learn how they speak their language in their natural environment. As a result of the limited number of learning options, traveling is the most effective method of learning a language. Learn to pronounce it correctly, or risk causing confusion and embarrassment in the future!

As a result, there will be fewer misinterpretations.

Take English for example. Even if they just acquire a basic form of the language, most non-native English speakers study English culture to better understand the meaning of the words they hear.

For outsiders, phrases and idioms like "it's raining cats and dogs" and "fly by the seat of your pants" would be difficult to decipher. In every language, you'll be able to locate similar instances.

Take it a step further. Even the English language itself reflects the diversity of the people who speak it. In countries where English is the primary language, outsiders may communicate in a variety of ways.

Distinct words have different connotations in different parts of the world, such as 'pants, biscuits, trainers, and football, for example. It might be difficult for English speakers to adjust to these nuances. Think about how difficult it would be for someone from a different culture!

It's not only English that has a variety of dialects. Make sure you're aware of cultural differences while you're studying it.

Language among Latin Americans varies greatly from country to country and even within Spain. In Argentina, 'boludo' signifies dumb, yet in Mexico, it can mean bold. While 'fresa,' in Spanish, refers to a strawberry, in Mexico, it could refer to a snob.

There is no difference between languages like French or Italian or Arabic or Chinese when it comes to this. Due to the ever-changing nature of languages, it is common for individuals to ascribe new meanings to familiar terms based on their own level of knowledge or geographic location.

To use the proper term in the right context, outsiders must understand cultural differences. There is less possibility for misinterpretation and confusion in this method.

Being multicultural makes it easier to learn a new language.

From an early age, we are open to absorbing other cultures. The method in which we process new information is influenced by the language we speak at home. As we mature, cultural contexts are vital for learning a new language.

It's a waste of time to learn a language without also learning about the culture that surrounds it.

Fried chicken or even fried vegetables without the proper seasonings for flavor, is kind of like eating lukewarm ice cream on a summer day.

It just doesn't taste like the 'real thang' without the necessary ingredients to make it edible and tasty.

You can eat it, but no one enjoys it.

With language it's the same way! If you just study from a language book. You'll learn about the recipe, but you won't be able to taste it.

If your only purpose of learning Chinese is to do business in China. Learn about the culture of China's people, their way of life, the foods they consume and the values and customs they hold dear in order to really understand the language. You'll get a fresh perspective on the language and learn it more quickly with the help of this information.

In order to THINK in a different language, you need to think ABOUT THE CULTURE.

A better understanding of the individuals you're speaking to might make it easier for you to communicate effectively. Rather than creating the phrases in your native language and then translating them into the new language, you will easily avoid having to do this at all.

Being able to think in a foreign language and understand the culture helps you to provide the proper meaning to each sentence you create.

English allows you to articulate ideas that would be impossible to convey verbatim in any other language. These things will become easier to explain when you comprehend cultural differences Between your native language, and your target language.

Learning a new language requires a deeper understanding of the culture that goes beyond just the surface level understanding. Learning a new language is easier if you have a better knowledge of the cultural context in which it is spoken. Without it, you'd be better off simply relying on a shaky machine translation.

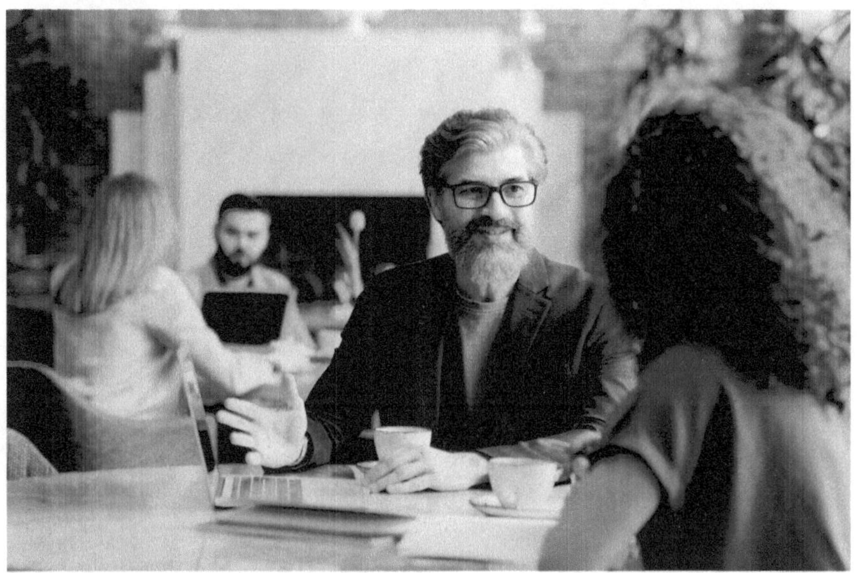

FINDING A TEACHER

You can do a lot of self-study when it comes to learning a language because of the wealth of information available on the Internet and language apps. However, if you want to become fluent in another language, you'll need to practice speaking with native speakers. This has the potential to be an issue in the past. However, we are fortunate to live in an age when we can communicate with individuals from all over the globe in a matter of seconds. To improve your communication skills, there's no better method than to engage in online sessions with others. To get the most out of your online sessions, we'll discuss how to choose a personal tutor or coach and offer you a few pointers.

- Use Your Teacher's Time Wisely.

Your online sessions should have clearly defined objectives. Will you primarily use a Language Coach to learn a new language? Or are you pursuing a different curriculum, such as the FLUENZ Immersion Experience, providing you with a more immersive experience to work on your communication abilities? If you know what you want to achieve, it may be easier to find a Personal Coach. There are a plethora of excellent tools available for anyone desiring to improve their language skills. Learning to speak out-loud in a language is an essential element of mastering any foreign language. Therefore, we recommend that students do as much of their learning as possible with the help of NueroLanguage Coaches. Most of your time with your Coach should be spent just speaking in your new language & helping you build bridges connecting the things you don't know to the things you already know, especially since that's the single thing you can't accomplish on your own.

- Don't Be Afraid to Speak Up during Class.

Say you choose a outdoor setting for your lesson or a small group session: Some coaches are a joy to listen to, but... Some language coaches really have a knack for getting you to open up and answer their questions. It's true that the discussion will be more challenging for you, but it also implies that you're making MORE progress. The ability to ask a lot of questions is essential for a language coach. You'll be fatigued by the conclusion of the hour-long session, but the amount of progress you'll make will be astounding. Express yourself naturally and speak as much as you possibly can in the discussion.

• Check to See if They're Good at Pointing Out Your Errors.

As far as we're concerned, finding a teacher that's perfectly balanced in all linguistic attributes is nearly impossible. However, one of the things that marks a really great language coach is the ability to balance HOW and WHEN to inform their pupils that they have said something incorrectly. Having a teacher constantly point out your mistakes might be frustrating and unproductive for some learners. A NeuroLanguage Coach can determine your skill level, your linguistic potential and point out the most crucial errors you make. Even the small ones you make over & over again. Additionally, you may assist your coach by letting them know whether they are correcting you too much or too little according to your preferences. And most importantly take advantage of your teacher's help.

• Selecting a Tutor or a Certified Language Coach

Tutors and Certified Language Coaches may be found on a few dedicated websites and apps specializing in how adult learners acquire & retain their target language. Two of which companies that are very reputable & clearly stand-out above the rest are Efficient Language Coaching & Fluenz.com.

Rachel Paling applies her many years of wisdom & experience as a multilingual professional Teachers and Coaches who have earned their certifications have more experience teaching and are often more qualified, but they can also be a little more expensive. Some tutors don't always have all the teaching experience outside of the internet, but they're still amazing at helping you improve your speaking abilities. Higher hourly rates aren't necessarily a sign of greater value, in our opinion. We think it's ideal to select a person with whom you have a strong connection. One of the best ways to tell if you've found the right coach is to engage in stimulating and engaging dialogue with them. If they help you to grow and progress, then we believe you are in the right place. There is no better way to learn a new language than to ENJOY the process of doing so.

- Finding the Right Teacher for Your Child Is Crucial.

The vast majority of Teachers on the learning platforms are excellent. Many professionals have various approaches, so it's best to test a few before making a final decision on which one is right for you.

That is the point at which it's time for you to develop your own ideas about what it takes to be a great Language Coach for you specifically. No matter what you do, make sure you're comfortable . Before your first class, you'll probably be apprehensive. Some people even decide to cancel the appointment due to the stress. This is very normal. If you can get past the first few moments of nervousness, you will find that a lot of it will subside once your session begins. As a learner, your coach should be able to calm you down and provide a calm, safe, brain friendly environment for learning. In order to keep things meaningful, refreshing, and enjoyable, make sure that you and your coach have something in common.

- Find Learning Methods that Work Best for You and Stick to Them.

If you choose to spend more time with multiple personal tutors, you will begin to discover what works best for you.

Ask your tutor to apply some of the strategies you've learned. Ask them to jot down some of the most critical errors you made throughout the session, and then have them assess your knowledge of those errors at the conclusion. For example, the tutor may notify you when you've made an error, but then let you work on it on your own to improve your fluency. I mean, think about it, even when you're speaking in your mother tongue, you'll still make a few basic blunders in a rapid discussion, even if you know how to say things properly. Often, when someone tells you the perfect way to express something, it can just pass right through your head. But when you have to stop and think about your errors and rectify them yourself using your own metacognition, you have a far higher chance of remembering them. That is part of what we call "brain friendly" learning!

It's good to experiment with different teaching methods to discover the ones that work best for you. Remember to speak out loud regularly and get comfortable with going outside of your comfort zone. That's the most important thing to remember.

In order to develop your speaking abilities, it is highly recommended that you engage in conversation with individuals from other parts of this beautiful planet we call home.

LEARNING FROM YOUR FAVORITE SHOWS

"Of all of our inventions for mass communication, pictures still speak the most universally understood language."

— WALT DISNEY

Now it's time to go even further outside of your comfort zone.

You're used to watching your favorite shows in your own language. As mentioned earlier, we're pretty comfortable on the sofa listening to our native tongue, as you should be. But if you want to master a new language, that same level of comfort needs to apply to the second (or third) language.

I'm talking about learning your new language from your TV shows and movies. And nowadays, that's not the only means of learning during your screen-time.

How much time do you spend on social media? Feel free to be honest, there's no (extreme) judgment here.

Most folks say "far too much time" when asked this question. Did you say that too?

It's not entirely surprising, either. We live in an era dominated by social media platforms. There are many individuals who have no idea how much time they spend reading through their news feeds each day. To learn a new language, you may start to fight against the pull of social media by limiting the amount of time you spend on it each day, or you can utilize it as a powerful friend to help you achieve your language goals.

USING SOCIAL MEDIA

Tossing a newcomer into an unfamiliar environment is like dropping a kid into the deep end of a pool, in the hopes that they would learn how to swim. In all likelihood, it won't. In your case, it may be a similar situation, AT THE BEGINNING you must not get too deeply involved in the complex grammar combinations, legal and medical jargon in your language or you may drown. Progression at a normal pace is essential for a total novice. The shallow end of the pool is the best place to begin your swim.

As a novice, creating your own immersion at home and selecting content that is appropriate for your current fluency level might be a more successful approach. You may want to begin with elementary-school-level content and work your way up the difficulty scale.

- Try the Audible App!

In order to learn a new language, listening to audiobooks is a great option since they enable you to add a lot of listening practice to your schedule and help you increase your weekly ratio of exposure. Whether walking the dog, traveling to work, or cleaning your home, you can listen to them while completing mundane repetitive tasks like household chores.

Many languages are included in Audible's vast collection of audiobooks. Finding audiobooks that are suited to your present proficiency in the language is a breeze. If you need to, you can even slow it down a little bit. Audiobooks may be purchased for as little as a few dollars and listened to as many times as desired. Take a break and immerse yourself at any moment.

- Get language exchange apps on your phone.

As previously said, you'll eventually want to engage in discussion with other individuals. Again, this is critical if you want to enhance your public speaking abilities. With the help of online language exchange, this may simply be accomplished. If you're looking to connect with other language learners from across the globe, italki and HiNative are great resources. Connecting with native speakers of the language you want to learn is really easy. While they're helping you learn their language, you may also help them learn yours.

If you'd like, you may hire a native speaker to tutor you on an hourly basis. As a result, you may devote all of your time to improving your speaking abilities out loud rather than aiding others. Your money, available time, and desired outcome all will come into play while making this decision.

- With YouTube, you can learn a new language in a fun way.

Every minute, an estimated 300 hours of video are posted to Youtube. There are 76 languages available for using YouTube. Almost every subject matter imaginable may be found on their site. There should be a video in your chosen target language. Find a subject title that interests you, translate it into your target language, then input it into YouTube. All of the videos are shown right away. As a YouTube user, you have access to a wide range of content on any subject that interests you.

Someone I know is a big fan of computer gaming. In his spare time, he likes watching Spanish gaming YouTubers. As a result, he's more comfortable conversing at the pace of native speakers, and at record speed too. There is no limit to what may be achieved. It's mind-boggling how much progress you can achieve when you're interested in a subject. Watching TED Talks and other conferences while studying languages is something I like doing as well.

- Make Friends on the Internet

I've talked about this possibility earlier in the book. NOW IS THE TIME! Don't be afraid to actually go for it! Your life will be forever changed by this decision. There are several benefits to having friends who are fluent in your target language. And many advantages to learning a new language in this way. You will open doors of opportunity with folks who communicate in ways that aren't always grammatically accurate but are still authentic, you'll learn a lot. When speaking, expect them to rely on colloquial language and odd idioms. In our courses, mentioned here in this book, you will learn about a foreign culture and HOW to apply the language in your daily life.

You'll be able to construct your own phrases from scratch after you've worked with them several times. You will often need to look up terms in your dictionary and be corrected by other native speakers when you misspeak while learning a new language.

It can be more motivating to keep going if you have internet buddies. You'll also want to maintain good participation in your lessons and practice your abilities in the wild, if you want to keep having engaging everyday discussions.

USING YOUR FAVORITE MOVIES

The idea that viewing movies may teach you a new language is probably not new to you. It is true that movies may be quite beneficial, but only if they are used as a learning tool. We'll show you how to use any movie as a teaching tool in this book.

- Start by watching the film in its original language (or mother tongue).

A movie you've seen a few times in English and are familiar with works best. The more acquainted you are with the film, the more you will get out of it. Seeing the movie at least once in English can help you comprehend what's going on if you haven't already.

Remember, children learn the FASTEST by hearing the language and SPEAKING OUT-LOUD through practice! Keep this in mind as you repeat the dialog & emotional expressions of your film or TV show. So now us adults can copy these kid's techniques to become fearlessly fluent in our languages FAST!

- Watch the movie in your target language AGAIN to ensure that you understand it.

Now that you've read the screenplay, go back and watch the movie again. In the early stages, it may seem like a waste of time to watch a movie more than once, but it is far more beneficial than seeing a number of movies just once. You'll learn a little more each time you study. As an alternative to seeing the movie on your desktop or TV, you might download it to your phone and listen to it while driving or exercising.

Even if you've seen the film before and are familiar with the plot, listening to the audio track may be just as informative as viewing it on the big screen. While driving, instead of listening to the radio, you may listen to the movie you just downloaded on your phone and enjoy a new learning experience.

- Find those recurring vocabulary words that you don't know by searching for them in the script.

After seeing the movie, you should have picked up quite a few new vocabulary words. However, you may not be able to memorize all of the new words that popped up repeatedly, even though you read or listened to the same ones over and over again. That's why it's a good idea to go back and reread the screenplay afterwards and check any unfamiliar terms you keep hearing. Now, what could you be thinking at this point?

The question you might be thinking is, 'Why now?" "Why didn't it occur to me the first time I read it?"

Even if you read the script and checked every single word in the dictionary before making any connections with it, the odds are that your brain just needs a little more time to taste the flavor of the new words, roll them around on your brain's figurative palette and then place them into their proper context. Even if you've seen the movie a few times and continued wondering what that strange term meant, you'll probably understand its significance better after a few viewings. Having a strong emotional attachment to something in the film definitely increases your chances of remembering what things mean later when you eventually check the dictionary. A single scene at a time may be quite effective for you as well. As soon as you've finished researching the words in a particular scenario, go back and re-listen to it again with the new information fresh in your mind.

- Watch it again, listen to it again.

If you rewatched the movie over again, you should have a good grasp on it now. The terms you looked up in the dictionary will be reinforced in this phase of the exercise. Reading the script or viewing the movie may continue until you are satisfied with your understanding of what was presented in the film.

Making an effort to follow these few procedures may have a significant impact on your learning journey, given the amount of text in a movie. With languages that are closely related to your mother tongue, and seeing that you're not a total novice, this strategy works well. You can now FEEL CONFIDENT that you are making PROGRESS and feel IN YOUR ABILITIES to grasp part of the language. While the first movie will be the most difficult and time-consuming, it will also be the most rewarding. You'll never forget it! 💪

FOR OUR NETFLIX USERS

Adults are excellent at learning languages when the learning sessions are interactive & engaging. There are several ways to learn a new language, including courses, flashcards, and fully immersive experiences at the executive level like a Fluenz In-Person Immersion Experience.

Now that you've been learning your foreign language for a while, have you ever noticed that as Native English Speakers we commonly overlook the importance of incorporating the language we've learned into our daily lives. The most effective language learners will do all they can to immerse themselves in the language. One of the best ways to achieve this is to watch a lot of television. Have you ever noticed how much TV you used to watch when you were a kid 😿? There are a number of places where you may access good quality material in your target language. Let me tell you, Netflix is the one and only magic word.

Netflix's expansion has been unmatched in the years following the release of the App Store. What a lot of language-learning material to devour! One of the best ways to incorporate a new language into your daily life is to watch TV and movies in that language. There are an expanding number of international episodes on Netflix, as well as a large number of translations & dubbed versions to aid you in your exploration. In this section of the book, we'll teach you how to utilize Netflix to brush up on your foreign language skills.

How to Locate Resources in a Foreign Language.

If you've ever attempted to learn a language by watching television, you know how difficult it can be to locate programming in your desired language. It's possible to check whether a title is available in a language other than English by selecting it and clicking on the language icon, even on Netflix.

Thanks to an easy-to-use tool, it is now possible to locate any show that is accessible in a certain language in either its original or dubbed form. In the address bar of your web browser, type in "netflix.com/browse/audio" or "netflix.com/browse/subtitles"

The language drop-down option will appear after logging in to your account. Simply choose your desired language from the drop-down menu. In this case, selecting "Korean" or "Spanish" from the drop-down option brings up a list of all titles available in that language.

It's an excellent idea to learn languages by watching films & TV, but only if you choose shows that are suitable for your present level of fluency. For someone who has just recently learned a new language, it's not worth it to sit down and watch a really sophisticated political drama. In most cases, you'll be unable to absorb all that legal terminology in an effective manner.

Streaming Dubbed Content You've Already Seen in the Original Language.

A word of caution… Sometimes the audio and subtitles won't always sync properly if they aren't closed captioned, and that can be quite confusing for the learner.

Select Reading Material Based on Your Current Level of Expertise.

Innumerable books are also accessible in a variety of languages. These titles may be used in many different ways. If you're just starting out, it's best to stick to books for younger readers. It's true what they say, "Never judge a book by its cover." You may be amazed at how much you may learn from the narrative, despite its childish appearance. Selecting content that is a little beyond your present level of proficiency in the language can help you improve your comprehension and fluency as well. In order for television to be valuable & useful for learning though, you need to spend more time studying the language. Especially if you struggle to even comprehend preschool episodes.

*Pro Tip:** Spend more time looking up words in your dictionary and even becoming more comfortable asking strangers for their thoughts on the meaning of a certain word or two that you would like more clarity on.

These moments of repeating childlike behavior, expressing your curiosity and wonder, taking time to ask strangers about the world around you, it's within these precious moments you are charging up your brain with massive amounts of linguistic energy, kind of like Goku in the Japanese anime series Dragon Ball Z. Then after your brain is charged up and ready to go all Super Saiyan, it can release that new vocabulary energy into newly formed sentences with people around you, at the market, at work, in the office or at the next family dinner 👄 where your Mother-In-Law is making your favorite dish. These moments spent in your dictionary & speaking with strangers are rocketing your fluency to the next level!!! 🚀

Watching Netflix series & films are a great method to immerse oneself in a new culture while learning a language. Your speaking abilities will develop dramatically if you incorporate Netflix as a reinforcer. Make the most of your newfound fluency by binge-watching some of your favorite series!

CHAPTER 6

BREATHE IN THE LANGUAGE & CULTURE TOGETHER

> *"Why, der language down dar in de far South is jus' as different from ours in Maryland, as you can think. Dey laughed when dey heard me talk, an' I could not understand 'dem, no how."*

— HARRIET TUBMAN

Do you feel that going too fast with your foreign language has the potential to hurt your progress just as much as going too slow?... Well, you're right. Whether you're pushing yourself too hard or not enough, you need to find that balance and learn how to BREATHE IN THE LANGUAGE.

Now, what does that mean?

Well, there are several different ways to look at it.

BABIES DON'T JUST LISTEN, THEY OBSERVE!

As kids are learning their mother tongue, we often think about just the words themselves as being absorbed in children's brains, along with the syntax and grammar of the language.

However, there is another essential part we often miss. Kind of like that old idiom "When you can't see the forest for the trees." Hehe, LOL… Sometimes a person can be so close to or focused on the few trees around them, they can miss all the other important things happening just around them that makes the forest function as a beautiful ecosystem.

One might even say that it comprises the very FOUNDATION of language itself!

It is BREATHING.

Yes, the inhales & exhales taken by the person speaking the language set the stage and are the very foundations upon which the sounds making up the person's language can now be built.

And this act of breathing is what the child, sitting "all comfy womfy" in its parent's arms, is observing intently! Not just the sounds coming out of the parent's mouth. But the very air itself.

- Dr. Patricia Kuhl, Co-Director of the Institute for Learning & Brain Sciences (I-LABS) at the University of Washington, has conducted extensive research on early language development. Her studies suggest that infants as young as six months old can discern the rhythmic patterns of speech, including the pauses for breath. According to Dr. Kuhl, this ability helps babies segment the continuous stream of speech into meaningful units, facilitating language acquisition.
- Dr. Laura Ann Petitto, a cognitive neuroscientist and Professor at Gallaudet University, has explored how infants use visual and auditory cues to acquire language. Her research indicates that babies pay close attention to the timing of adults' breathing during speech, suggesting that breathing patterns serve as important cues for language learning from the earliest stages of development.
- Dr. Daniel Amen, a psychiatrist and brain imaging specialist, has explored the neural mechanisms underlying language processing. His research suggests that areas of the brain involved in breathing regulation, such as the brainstem and cerebellum, are closely interconnected with regions responsible for language comprehension and production. This connection underscores the integral role of breath in the neural networks supporting spoken language.

Research into the differences in breathing patterns across languages sheds light on the fascinating interplay between language and physiology. Here are some insights into how languages like Spanish, English, German, and Chinese exhibit distinct breathing patterns:

Spanish vs. English:

- Ever noticed how Spanish sounds so smooth and rhythmic? Well, that's because Spanish tends to stress each syllable more evenly. Picture it like a smooth ride on a paved road. You know exactly when to take a breath because the stress is predictable.
- But English? It's like a rollercoaster of stress! Sometimes you're cruising smoothly, and suddenly, bam! Stress hits you out of nowhere. That unpredictability can make breathing a bit more erratic.

German vs. Chinese:

- German, with its long compound words, is like a linguistic marathon. Speakers often take deeper breaths to power through those lengthy phrases. It's like gearing up for a long hike in the mountains!
- Now, Mandarin Chinese adds another twist with its tonal nature. Imagine trying to balance delicate objects while walking a tightrope. Mandarin speakers need precise breath control to nail those tone changes without toppling over.

These differences aren't just quirks of language; they're reflections of each culture's unique rhythm and style. So, the next time you're learning a new language, pay attention to how your breathing changes. It's not just about words; it's about syncing up with a whole new rhythm of life!

You see, it is your breath that sets the tone for each language spoken. It is the backbone of our linguistics. Yes, our breathing forms the structure for all the intricate framework that comes with speaking OUR FIRST LANGUAGE. So naturally and effortlessly do we match the breathing styles of those around us as a child, we barely notice it's even there.

Breath dictates the cadence & rhythm of the words used. And can even provide the space to give meaning to the gaps & pauses in the air, when there are no words uttered at all.

So please allow this nugget of newborn wisdom to be a key ingredient for you soaking up your new foreign tongue. Observe the breathing styles of the native speakers around you!

This "kid's stuff" is common knowledge amongst babies. You can almost see them whispering their secrets to fast fluency in each other's ears as they play, crawl and laugh on the playground. As the adults sit literally & figuratively on the outside, on the sidelines as it were, just out of reach of the children's secret club, for "members only" right. For us adults these "Secret Golden Keys to Fluency" have been hiding right in plain sight!... Which can now become our door leading to ⚡ LIGHTNING FAST FLUENCY.

TAKE YOUR TIME

Native speaker speed is one of the most difficult aspects of learning a new language. Native speakers frequently communicate at a pace that is impossible for a novice to understand, regardless of the language they are speaking. This may seem counterintuitive, but SLOW PRONUNCIATION IS KEY and can be very beneficial in your early stages. To assist you in better comprehending native speakers, the OUINO & CHINESEPOD applications have everything recorded at two different pronunciation speeds. Also the FLUENZ app & website has everything you need, and is uniquely tailored to your specific desired results, including your fluency at different pronunciation speeds out in the wild.

- Reducing the Speed of All Online Videos.

There is an excellent tool for helping to control the speed of your videos. It works in Brave and Firefox and is named "Video Speed Controller." All of your videos will now have choices in the upper left corner once you've installed the app. The speed may be reduced by 10% steps. Find a pace that works best for you and stick with it. You can even view your favorite series and movies in slow motion on Netflix.

- Audiobooks should be slowed down.

In most applications, you can buy audiobooks in the language you're studying and slow them down to your preferred pace, such as on Audible. Slowing down recordings of basic audiobooks may be quite beneficial for beginners. To further enhance your vocabulary, you may be amazed how many new words your brain will acquire by listening to an audiobook of a narrative YOU ALREADY KNOW.

REALISTIC VOCABULARY GOALS

As a general rule, people are curious about the length of time it takes to learn a new language. It's almost hard to answer this question without a lot of guesswork. "What If's." A better comparison would be asking how long it takes to master the guitar. There are just too many variables at play to provide a definitive solution.

Start with the basic words.

Words like "apple" and "vehicle" are indisputable examples of simple vocabulary items that anybody can pick up quickly. Just like when you were a kid! These words don't require several instances in various contexts to be comprehended. With a simple visual or translation, your brain can easily associate the new word with its sound & meaning.

Fortunately, the majority of terms aren't that difficult to understand. Some may take a little longer to master, but the payoff can be enormous! Making the additional time and effort to whip out your dictionary to LOOK UP YOUR NEW VOCABULARY around you very worthwhile.

The "Beginner" lessons on the Chinesepod App are a great place to find several of these terms.

The world of conjugating verbs.

Here's a good question, when is the last time you have ever seen a kid on the playground counting verbs? While conjugations aren't words per se, they're an essential skill to master. Trust me.

Regular verb conjugation opens the door to a smorgasbord of fresh vocabulary. It's critical to realize that mastering another language entails much more than just memorizing a slew of vocabulary.

Understanding that what seems like extra "body parts" to us, hanging off the side of their language, is actually serving as an essential tool bonded to the very structure of their language, allowing them to express themselves openly & freely, this realization is worth its weight in gold.

These are the things you need to take your time with learning. Plan each session (for how many days of the week you see yourself working on these concepts). Don't get overwhelmed. Missing a planned day isn't going to set you back. The most important step is consistency. Keep your sessions short if you know time is an issue.

What does it mean to master a word?

Just one more thing to keep in mind. The only way to completely grasp a word is to speak it, read it and write it. What if you can already get the gist of it in a quick exchange with others? Remember, it is only when you can use it without thinking, that you actually understand it like a native.

In Spanish , "manzana" is the term for "apple." Now that you know what that means, is that all you need? Well, if you don't reinforce it, you'll likely forget it in no time. Now, when you envision the image of this yummy piece of fruit, the Spanish word may just start to pop into your mind from now on. I wonder how long it will take until the term "manzana" pops up as the 1st word for you and is as well-known as "apple." When you think of the Spanish term now, you'll think of a small figurative seed that has just been sown in your heart 🩶.

If you take a Fluenz Course, for example, you will have learned and used the term in a variety of contexts by the conclusion of your course. Healthy and well-rooted, these expressions will be. However, if you just read a word in the dictionary, and tried repeating it, the word may still be delicate in your memory, and if you learn a new phrase and never use it again, it can disappear quickly. Regardless of the methods you use to master them. However, the words will naturally get stronger over time if you are continually exposed to the language in various ways. You shouldn't be concerned about forgetting since forgetting it's a normal part of the learning process. Even if you can't recall the new words you've learned, they're still lodged someplace in your brain. A new lesson, a TV program, a book, or any other place you frequent, your new language will bring it back to the surface and help you remember it.

The key is to sow robust vocabulary seeds in your brain, water them regularly, and expose them to plenty of sunlight. Then sit back and watch your FLUENCY grow. You have heard about learning a new word or new phrase each day on your path to fluency, right? Ah haaa... But, remember to maintain your other linguistic gardens of progress you have already cultivated for at least a few minutes a day, which only needs a few more seeds and a little more cultural exposure to truly take off now and grow luxuriantly... And guess what? Your garden is beginning to look so nice! Native speakers will be complimenting you in no time! 😘

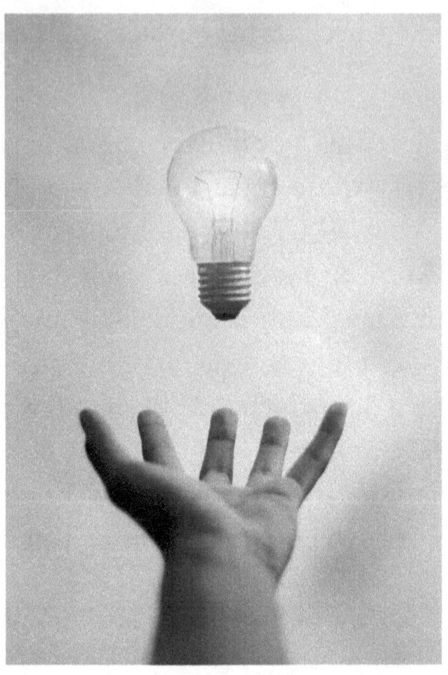

🔥 Dive Deeper into the World of Language with FluentBrain.Me Online Courses! 🔥

———

Hey, Fellow Language Adventurer! 🌍✈️

Firstly, a hearty virtual pat on the back for coming this far in our enlightening book! By now, you're on your way to discovering the "5 FluentBrain Habits" later in the book and are well on your way to becoming a linguistic superstar. But guess what? This is just the beginning of our journey together.

If you've got that spark, that fire, that insatiable hunger to not just learn but *master* your target language, then, my friend, it's time to turn up the heat and cook up a linguistic storm.

Why Take the Next Step with FluentBrain.Me?

- Exclusive Content: Dive into a treasure trove of resources – from interactive lessons, immersive exercises, fun quizzes, and so much more, curated by linguistic experts.
- Tailored Learning Paths: We recognize and celebrate your individuality. With FluentBrain.Me, enjoy courses crafted just for *you,* suiting your pace and style.
- Connect with Native Coaches: It's like having a friend from every corner of the world! Our native coaches are here to guide, support, and share inside secrets of the language and culture.
- Community Vibes: Join a global community of passionate learners. Exchange stories, practice together, and cheer each other on. We're more than a platform; we're a kinship.

Real Stories from Real People:

"FluentBrain.Me transformed my linguistic journey. The courses are interactive, engaging, and the community is so supportive!"

— WENDY M.

"I've tried many platforms, but FluentBrain.Me stands out. It's personalized, comprehensive, and so much fun. I highly recommend it!"

— JEREMY H.

____

Special Offer JUST For You! 🎁

Because you've been a spectacular companion through this book journey, we've got a sweet deal waiting. Sign up now, become a client and get a 20% discount on your courses! Yes, you read that right!... Just use code: **MYFLUENT20** to get 20% off your first purchase today!

____

But Wait, There's More! 🌈

The first 100 sign-ups will receive an exclusive bonus, "FluentBrain's Guide to Cultural Nuances & Taboos" – an indispensable tool as you navigate the vast oceans of language and culture.

____

Are You Ready to Ignite Your Path To Great Results? 🔥

The world is vast, diverse, and waiting for you to explore it. With FluentBrain.Me, you're not just learning words and grammar; you're embracing cultures, forging global friendships, and setting your FLUENCY on the path to SUCCESS.

Don't just stand by as a spectator. Discover your hidden "Superpower" within your BRAIN and be a real hero in the story of your own life. Dive into the deeper, more vibrant layers of your language-learning journey.

Join FluentBrain.Me NOW and Elevate Your Linguistic Game! 🚀

Click Here & Begin Your FluentBrain Adventure!

———

P.S. Remember, language isn't just about communication. It's about connection. At FluentBrain.Me, we're here to make sure every word you utter, every sentence you form, resonates and connects. Dive in and watch your world expand!

Don't Just Speak. Connect. 🌍🤍🗣️

KEEP YOUR EARS ON

"Learning a new language is not just about learning new vocabulary or grammar rules; it's about using your hands to weave YOUR OWN story, it's about understanding the SOUL of the language, the culture, and connecting with the HEART of the people."

— *RYAN JOHNSON*

Some would say this is the hardest part. Why? Because we're so used to our native tongue, we prefer hearing it for most of our day. We're most comfortable with it. Our foreign language study can be just a hobby sometimes, or at least we can treat it that way at times.

In order to master another language, we need to keep our ears open to it whenever possible.

A language teacher from Language Arts Academy, Liz Bertrand, has a very captivating view of how to get the most out of your foreign language with your ears.

To produce great results, you can make sure the language you're trying to learn may be heard in the background at all times (Bertr, 2017).

Listening to a podcast, the radio, or a TV program in your target language while going about your everyday tasks is simple, even if you're busy. Learning to recognize the PACE, INTONATION , and FREQUENT PHRASES used by native speakers is the objective here.

Setting clear and quantifiable objectives is a great way to keep track of your progress.

It's important to keep in mind that the objectives you set for yourself will vary based on your expertise with the language and how acquainted you are with the topic matter.

To get you started, she has a few great suggestions:

- Make a list of 10 new terms or phrases you learned while watching a foreign film.

Fill in the blanks as you listen to a song in the language you are studying to identify a news issue and find out what native speakers of the language have to say about the subject.

- Get yourself ready before you listen.

Spend a few moments contemplating what you're going to listen to next. What do you already know about the topic? What are some key terms or phrases that you would want to remember? Which media will you be using to entertain yourself? Are there any jokes that you like?

Are there any new TV Shows or any Radio Shows that interest you? If so, what do you hope to learn from them?

In order to improve their listening abilities, it has been shown that students benefit most by devoting time to thinking about their expectations before listening, checking to see whether the information meets those expectations while listening, and then measuring their understanding afterward.

Then, listen again.

You'll be shocked at how much more you have picked up each time you listen to the same audio again..!

There is a gradual change in how the language you hear sounds over time.

- Keep a running tab of new words and phrases that you learn.

Whenever you hear anything you don't recognize, write it down phonetically and take note of the circumstances around it. In this manner, you can go back and check it up later or ask someone knowledgeable about the subject (such as a language coach or native speaker). Look it up in your dictionary right away if possible.

- Seek out opportunities to interact with people.

Practice is the greatest method to learn. When you have the chance, try to communicate with people who are native speakers of the language. If you're looking for firms that cater to or are popular among native speakers, look into them. Learn the language just like children, by conversing with those who are fluent in the language you're studying.

ENGAGE IN ACTIVE LISTENING

In other words, what can you do to increase your foreign language listening comprehension?

Viewing movies with subtitles, listening to podcasts or music, sitting in a café while listening to the conversations happening around you in real-time or even watching the local news in the language you're studying are some of the most common ways to practice "keeping your ears on" amongst native speakers. Is there anything more you might be doing to be more proactive and more effective? You can find out by following our advice in the next section!

Active listening has also helped me tremendously to become a fluent speaker in multiple languages. At the beginning of my language journey, I used the routine of listening to "the Pimsleur Tapes", as they were affectionately called. These were the audio recordings made for beginners to help you actively listen to your target language… Just like children do when they actively listen in their mother tongue.

I can remember listening to the recordings and repeating the words with the exact tone, pitch, and pace of the native speaker. It was fun and exciting, because I could see my progress as I advanced through the lessons… I would even try out the new phrases that I learned from the recordings "in the wild" as I would meet other native speakers during the day. Maybe at a coffee shop, at the grocery store, while doing the laundry or while walking my dog in the park.

It was an excellent way for me to get feedback and improve my pronunciation. Also, it didn't cost me any extra money because the Pimsleur Language recordings were free to check out at my public library, and no one ever charged me for speaking to them in their native tongue while at the grocery store… Lol

Making progress and becoming more fluent is an unforgettable feeling and it will actually change your life. To best help you, there were a few things that I noticed as keys to my success. I also noticed that when other language learners failed to do these few simple things, their progress started to decline and they even gave up on learning their new language.

#1 was repeating the words OUT LOUD. Yes, actually getting the words out of my mouth was the KEY 🔑 . That's right, actually speaking the words out loud was a HUGE advancement toward my fluency!

Generally, the people that don't repeat the words or speak the words out loud tend to lose focus and struggle with making progress.

#2 was making time to speak to other native speakers and receive feedback. Native speakers provide immediate feedback to you, activating your reward center of the brain, and helping you to make corrections where needed. Native speakers also connect you to the culture of your target language, helping you make connections that are otherwise not possible. This improves your fluency by leaps and bounds.

Along with surrounding yourself with passive listening, please remember to ENGAGE IN ACTIVE LISTENING as well. The author of Fluency Made Achievable, Kerstin Hammes, offers some excellent tips on how to be a more active listener.

- Play it again.

This task is good for those who are starting to spend a great many hours immersed in foreign language audio and video content, as I've mentioned earlier. This exercise will slash through all of your rationalizations and lapses in concentration. Get into the habit of pausing what you're listening to every now & then while listening to those recordings. Put yourself in the shoes of the performers and pretend you're being asked about the subject matter they were discussing on-screen. When you're watching a drama, put yourself in the action by imagining you're there. What are your thoughts? What are your thoughts on these points?

Do not only envision what you would say but respond to the video or the characters in your brain. Speak as though no one is listening. This is a great study aid to have on hand whether driving or doing homework somewhere. Instead of avoiding the conversation, you will be compelled to participate. To really grasp what is being said, it is necessary to listen intently and respond thoughtfully when you feel compelled to do so. There will be no more evasions of effort.

- Defining your personality.

When Hammes interviewed language learner David Mansaray for her book, she was told that he likes using a foreign language to explain what he sees and hears (Hammes, 2015). You may say something like, "The child is wearing his hat," or "The lady is walking with a pram," or "I like to think in a foreign language when I feel the people around me are a bit uninteresting." This is an activity I can do at any time, any place. Aside from practicing, it also helps me uncover vocabulary and grammar structures I need to improve on. I keep track of these ideas in a tiny notepad that I keep in my bag and return to them later to work on them.

When it comes to utilizing your language, it doesn't matter whether you're recording it on your phone or writing it down in a notebook, as David does. You don't have to limit yourself to vocabulary lists in a foreign language. Feel free to branch out to raising questions, idioms, local phrases, or even memes. What matters most is that you use the language often, and that you create something in it. To help you transition out of the honeymoon period, this activity is very beneficial since it helps to form new habits quickly, which may make a tremendous impact on your progress.

- Every day, jot down a few lines.

When it comes to learning a new language, writing is an essential component. Writing makes you pay attention because you have to pay attention to what you're saying. While writing anything on your phone, you're unable to see what's happening on the television. Writing has a way of telling you something about yourself "Look at this!... This is the area on which you should concentrate your efforts at the moment "

As a matter of fact,. I often discuss how much I believe this practice is underappreciated, yet it is the quietest essential language competency. If you're an extrovert or want to overcome your shyness by learning a new language, you may not be able to devote hours to writing short tales.

Short and frequent writing practice is still recommended. A line a day requires just five minutes of your time each day, yet it has a greater impact on your life than listening to half an hour of podcasts. If you have a tutor or coach, consider sending them emails or texts in your target language every now and then.

Alternatively, you might begin by translating a single sentence a day from your native language to your target language. As you realize you've written thousands of words in a foreign language, you'll experience a tremendous feeling of accomplishment. Keep your eyes peeled for the treasure when it arrives, and give yourself a well deserved pat on the back for a job well done.

MORE ACTIVE LISTENING ACTIVITIES

You'll be able to keep up with native speakers like never before with the aid of these listening exercises.

- Summarize!

To improve your language abilities, make notes on what you've learned while watching French television or listening to Spanish radio.

Agnieszka Murdoch of 5-Minute Language demonstrates that summarizing may improve both listening and speaking abilities. It's easy to get ready for a summarizing exercise by playing a short program (30 minutes or less) and listening to it twice. Listen intently and attempt to absorb as much as you can in the first round of the session. Pause the video if you're having problems understanding what's being said. Try to jot down significant ideas and topics for the second round.

In either a written or spoken summary, summarize what you've learned from these two rounds of listening. It's a terrific method to work on listening and vocabulary at the same time, and summarizing is a great way to practice both.

- Get material that varies in length.

Maintain your interest in the learning process by listening to several types of programs. Shorter information like podcasts and lengthier content like audiobooks may be used in conjunction, according to language expert Steve Kaufmann.

Because you'll be listening to them for weeks or months at a time, you'll find that longer materials are more relaxing and steady. This might help you establish a habit and give you something to look forward to. The text version of the audiobook could be easier to come by if you decide to go that way. Set aside time after listening to go through the questions you've written to ensure you've understood all that was said. While you're at it, review transitions and filler words to improve your sentence structure and comprehension.

The Benefits of Studying in the Evenings.

I've talked about studying during the day. What about studying at night?

Studying before going to bed can definitely be a more efficient way to learn a language. Those who study within the eight hours before going to sleep are more likely to perform well on tests, according to research. Getting some shut-eye may help you organize your thoughts better too. Whether you choose the Fluenz Language Immersion program or another method, completing one language lesson each night before you go to bed can provide impressive benefits. As a bonus, you won't have to deal with the constant droning of sounds throughout the night. It's better to focus on spending your waking hours as efficiently as possible and ensure that you get a decent night's sleep in order to recuperate after a hectic day. That's just our humble opinion.

CHAPTER 8

HOW TO STOP PROCRASTINATING

"Procrastination is like a credit card: it's a lot of fun until you get the bill."

— CHRISTOPHER PARKER

You've worked so hard for this, the moment when you've finally laid out your schedule for studying your target language. You have your notebooks, websites, language apps, and even your meeting with your friend / language coach to help out is happening later this week. You're excited to finally learn the language that'll help you now, for that family trip coming up soon and for that fancy career in the future. You know the doors that'll open right up when you will soon reach fluency. And you know there's nothing stopping you from doing it.

You're feeling so confident about this new start. And it's looking so promising.

But that was three days ago.

You've been staring at that notebook for some days now. Those flashcards are still neatly stacked on your desk, waiting for your 10 minute session of review. You text your friend / coach earlier this morning to push the date back to some unknown time because you're feeling pretty tired today.

You also want to catch up on your sleep and do some chores later, then maybe hang out with some friends later that night.

Those very same reasons continue on for some more days, which turn to weeks, and before you know it, it's been three months! The clutter has long since buried your study material somewhere in the room.

Do you know what I'm describing here? It's procrastination.

But guess what? YOU CAN defeat procrastination. It doesn't have to dominate your language studies. All you have to do is take it one step at a time.

Our company's philosophy is as follows:

 *"Babies learn languages like ants eat elephants."*

— FOUNDER OF FLUENTBRAIN.ME

We believe that little moments of progress each day compound through the USE of your new language. And in no time at all, you look around and see just how far you have come. It's just like collecting precious stones on an all-day hike and finally reaching the top of the mountain. When you turn around to look out over the hills & valleys, looking way out into the distance, you can see where you started your journey and all the massive progress that you have made. Instead of aiming for fluency super quickly, maybe you can just focus on everyday growth. Be grateful for the little victories along the way, just like precious gemstones ◈.

Create a routine you can stick to, and never give up! A new language may be a delight to learn from the very beginning, if you redefine what it means to become fluent in your mind.

Let's walk through this.

TAKING THE RIGHT STEPS

Many elements come into play while trying to learn a new language, but maybe the most critical is your own personal drive to succeed. If you're willing to put in the effort, you'll definitely find a way. Motivated learners not only ENJOY THE PROCESS more, but they also learn more quickly and more efficiently than those who aren't.

You can't stay inspired 24 hours a day, seven days a week, no matter how determined you are. People postpone because they are exhausted, overwhelmed with work and responsibilities, or just because they don't feel like it. On the other hand, procrastination is a skill that we humans have honed to a fine art over years of practice. Procrastination and a lack of desire may have a significant impact on your ability to learn a language, if not nipped in the bud right away.

Why do we put things off till the last minute?

It's okay to procrastinate from time to time; it's not harmful. However, if you often put off studying and practicing your goal language because you are too busy procrastinating, it's time to do something! But first, let's examine some of the possible causes of your procrastination.

- Distractions Aplenty / Inappropriate Settings
- Unknown Objectives
- Minimal Effort For One's Results
- Failures In The Past
- Having A Lot of Tension or Exhaustion
- Perfectionism
- Anxiety Over Becoming Unsuccessful
- Recognizing The Difficulty of The Job
- Various Other Concerns
- A Lack of Drive

Distractions should be minimized by recognizing and eliminating them.

If you were born with a smartphone in your hand, it's more simple than ever to become sidetracked. In the midst of all the things you have to do each day, there always seems to be something else you can be doing. For example, even seemingly innocuous tasks, such as cleaning the dishes, or feeding the dog might distract you from your educational goals.

Consider the surroundings. Make an effort to identify and minimize the items that most easily cause you to get distracted. In the absence of streaming services like Netflix or Disney+ that are specifically designed to help you improve your foreign language skills, consider turning off your phone's alerts, putting your device on Airplane Mode, hitting the focus button, which allows you to remain distraction-free for a set amount of time, or putting it away altogether, as well as delegating some of your responsibilities. Make a study area, in your home or office, if you can. Even if you have a desk at home, it might be anywhere as simple as your bedroom floor to a quiet place on the lawn. Leave your house and study at a park, the library, or a café if you want. Having fewer distractions will allow you to focus better on your studies.

- Concentrate on what you studied before!

You might get demotivated if it seems like you're not making any progress. Reflecting on what you've accomplished in the past might be really beneficial in this situation.

See what you've previously studied in your language-learning app's previous books or levels. Find past notes and activities you've completed and review them. Take a look at the materials you've already read in your target language. Seeing how far you've progressed will give you a sense of how simple it was to learn the preceding topics.

In order to practice your target language, sit down with a piece of paper or note-taking software and compose a piece of writing on any subject you want. To begin, you will be surprised at how much information you already own. As a bonus, it will serve as a reminder to yourself in the future when you run over another bump in the road on your quest for fluency.

- Celebrate your victories and reward yourself for them.

Having a sense of accomplishment isn't always enough. Rewarding yourself for your accomplishments is a great way to keep yourself motivated.

It's important to recognize and appreciate both significant and minor accomplishments. Traveling the world after passing a difficult language test is undoubtedly inspiring, but you don't have to travel all the way across the world to reap the rewards of a successful learning session.

- Keep in mind WHY you began in the first place.

When we are immersed in the daily grind of school, jobs, and simply getting by, it's easy to lose sight of why we started out in the first place. When and why did you begin studying your target language? Finding your initial passion for studying the language will help you get back on the right track. Were you motivated to learn the language because it runs in your family? Are your relatives & In-Laws native Spanish speakers? Are you planning a vacation soon and want to be sure you're well-prepared to connect with the locals?

- Set objectives that are both hard and attainable.

To go anywhere quickly, you need to know where you're going. For language learning, this is true too. If you don't have a clear goal in mind, you may make slower, less consistent progress and find it more challenging to remain motivated.

Smaller objectives, such as finishing a 45-90 minute lesson on your FLUENZ APP, are just as significant as larger ones, like obtaining a new level or reading a whole chapter in a book. Make sure the objectives are intriguing and difficult to achieve. They must also be grounded in reality. Avoid aiming for fluency in a matter of days or weeks by establishing unrealistic objectives. Setting unachievable objectives is a surefire way to lose motivation and set yourself up for failure. Self-love is the most important thing you can do.

The goal of learning a language is not to arrive at a certain point in a certain amount of time.

- Be a stickler for rules while being open-minded & curious.

To be able to recall and learn new information, we need to EXERCISE YOUR BRAINS on a regular basis.

Developing and sticking to a language review schedule that is uniquely tailored to your needs will not only help you maintain focus, but it will also make it simpler to build fluency on a regular basis. You won't even think about it, just like brushing your teeth before going to sleep, since it will become a habit. Routine activities take less mental work than those that are not part of your daily routine.

Then, it's also vital to give oneself a break from time to time. For whatever reason, you may not be able to study on a certain day.

When this occurs, don't be hard on yourself. If at all feasible, make up for what you've missed in future sessions before returning to your usual study schedule.

- Build your internal drive to succeed.

The process of learning a foreign language may be fueled by a variety of factors, and combining them can speed up the process even more.

Advancing your career could be motivating you to learn a new language. Then, think of all the other advantages it provides: better and more real travel experiences, access to hidden knowledge never available to you before, and the chance to meet new people from all over our beautiful globe. Finally enjoying the ability to speak to your family members, maybe even your extended family including your mother-in-law or father-in-law that takes such good care of you whenever you visit them. Speaking to them in their native tongue could bring you closer together in a way you never experienced before, you will learn so much about their life & their history. This may be another motivation for you. You probably can think of a number of reasons why you want to learn a new language, then hold on tight, because your progress will now be stratospheric!

- Vary the tools and resources you use to learn a language.

I cannot overemphasize this nugget of wisdom enough! Not only can studying from a single source be tedious, but it may actually harm your ability to learn. If you want to learn a new language, you'll need more than one resource. Some language learning applications, for example, concentrate only on vocabulary rather than grammar. Others don't involve speech practice.

A key takeaway from these examples is the need to immerse yourself in the language in a variety of contexts. As a result, each study session will be more fruitful.

- Eat healthily and relax when you can.

Were you aware that a lack of motivation might be caused by a lack of sleep or enough nutrition? Your brain and body both need nutrition and relaxation in order to digest your new language effectively.

Take a break from studying if you're feeling especially worn out. Stay healthy by eating correctly, working out regularly, and getting enough sleep. When we sleep our brains re-enforce what we've learned.

- Take a walk or run in the fresh air.

Long periods of time spent inside or at a computer aren't beneficial to your health, in fact, they can be counterproductive to your education. It's possible to acquire cabin fever, boredom, or distraction when you're stuck indoors all day.

Exercising regularly has been shown to improve memory in studies (We will speak more thoroughly about this later in the book.). Walking or working out at home may help you get rid of surplus energy, boost your endorphins, and enhance your attention & focus. Additionally, it's a terrific method to get your mind off of the stress at the office and return to it later with a new set of eyes.

- Make an effort to live your life in your chosen language.

No matter how good your Coach or Instructor is, or how well-equipped you are, learning a language may still be a bear at times. It is essential that you continue to learn the language on a regular basis, preferably daily. This may be remedied by finding methods to make learning a language a part of your everyday routine. The benefit of this strategy is that you can continue to work on your language skills even if you miss a scheduled learning session. It won't even feel like you're learning if you do it correctly, which is a welcomed change!

Is any of your daily routine or the content you consume possible to get in your target language? Use the internet and your favorite television programs to review the previous chapter. This is an essential component of getting to know your new language on a daily basis.

- Set a time limit for yourself.

Setting a deadline is a good idea if you have trouble staying motivated. You may perform better when you have a deadline to meet. The old adage that "work expands to fill the time allotted," also known as "Parkinson's Law," suggests that if you give yourself a specific (and realistic) deadline to accomplish a task, you'll likely succeed. Set a new objective after achieving the first one.

As an example, one may think of a language-level test. You may use these tests as a guide for your learning route, as well as a precise timeline since they generally outline the anticipated levels of competency.

If tests aren't your thing, look for a language-learning event in your region (or online) and get yourself ready to go. Nevertheless, remember to keep your objectives in perspective and allow yourself enough time to prepare, depending on the occasion and your degree of proficiency in the target language.

- Mistakes are part of the learning process, so accept them and move on.

It may seem strange at first, but making errors is an integral part of the process of learning a new language. In order to grow, we must make errors.

The fear of making mistakes is a common anxiety among adult learners, who are terrified of sounding dumb, being judged, or being laughed at by others if they make a mistake. To their detriment, we find they prefer not to speak at all. People often assume that youngsters are better at learning since they don't experience the kind of anxiety that adults do. Which is why many adults have raised their hands and asked us to step in to help them make progress. Becoming FLUENTLY CONFIDENT as a result.

Procrastination for some learners can be downright crippling, due to this lingering fear of making errors. Which, by the way, is another great reason not to postpone THE JOY OF YOUR MOMENT, when you want to speak what you're thinking out loud in a group of your friends & family. Because, without speaking out loud, you won't really know whether you're on the right track if you don't try it out in a public setting. (This is one of the secret weapons kids use to become fluent on the playground with their friends around them… Remember?)

- From the beginning, speak your language OUT-LOUD.

Over the years, my experience becoming fluent in multiple languages has saved me countless times from frustration, from embarrassing situations & has saved me so much valuable time picking up my next language. My advice to new learners and my advice to you is, begin speaking your target language AS SOON AS you begin to study it. Just say what you know, no matter where you are in the learning process. Even if you just learn a few words, practice them out loud or in conversation. Make it a point to train your brain 🧠 on a daily basis. Your abilities will improve, you'll have more fun, and your procrastination will be removed over time as you are more active.

- Focus on what works and what doesn't, in order to improve your progress.

As you walk through this book picking up all of these "golden nuggets" I'm gently laying at your feet, it's important to keep in mind that each one of us has a unique way of learning. As such, even the best materials at your fingertips may not work for everyone. If they happen not to be a good fit for your particular needs, daily routine or learning style, please remember it doesn't make them terrible in nature nor does it make you a failure.

Because there are so many linguistic tools and methods available out there, it's critical to avoid wasting time or energy on those that don't connect with you. No matter what the newest fad may be. Make an honest evaluation of your own learning process: what works and what doesn't, what areas of the language arouse your interest, which type of media you like, and what produces the best outcomes for you. Because no one knows you better than you.

- Visualize yourself succeeding.

In order to succeed with anything in life, including language fluency, it's a good idea to use visualization methods. With the aid of visualization, it becomes easier to take the essential steps toward achieving your goals.

Imagine what your life will feel like after you've mastered the language you're learning. What benefits have you enjoyed on a daily basis? Do you work in a language-related field for your career? How does this new life feel around you? Traveling has now become easier for you. Who have you made new connections with? Does part of your family speak a different language? Can your mother-in-law or father-in-law understand you when you tell them the story of how you fell in love & met the love of your life?

Imagining your future success may be a great source of inspiration. Create a vision board, both IRL and virtual, to help you see your future. Fill it with phrases in your target language, photographs of locations you will visit, family gatherings, and anything else you identify with your success in learning the language, anything that makes you feel like you're making progress.

This vision board may serve as a constant source of inspiration and encouragement as you work toward achieving your language journey to fluency.

- Avoid blaming yourself for the challenges you're experiencing.

It's not easy to pick up a new language. Keep in mind that it's normal to feel this way. To blame oneself would just lead to a torrent of negative energy & ideas that would be counterproductive to your developmental progress. Acknowledge, accept, and then devise a strategy for coping with every problem you may be faced with, whether personal or language-related. Reach out to a friend, a partner, or a member of Fluentbrain.Community. NEVER give up! Keep learning and practicing.

- Don't get caught up on the outcome; rather, focus on the journey!

Obsessing over your progress is counterproductive, no matter what your motivations are for learning a language. This may seem great at first: the top test score in your class, the perfect score on your language-learning software, or a faultless completion of an activity.

You NEED BOTH short-term goals and long-term goals WORKING TOGETHER to truly be successful.

Otherwise, you may be less likely to remember what you've learned. Does your life depend on how many questions you get correct on the exam? What happens if you don't? That kind of pressure can be a dangerous move.

If you want to learn a new language successfully, concentrate on the JOURNEY & the PROCESS rather than the product: ENJOY what you are doing and SAVOR the small moments when you speak the language fluently. Having a perfect score isn't as crucial as being able to communicate effectively with native speakers in the wild. Nice, smooth fluency in your new language will follow automatically if you concentrate on the process.

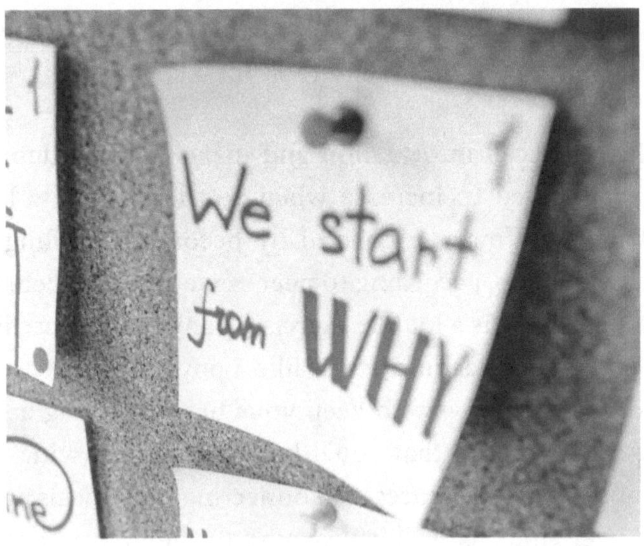

"I'M JUST NOT MOTIVATED ANYMORE"

No one can deny the rising prominence & influence of the English language over our globe. So what's the use of learning a foreign language if you can communicate in English in most countries?" Why study a foreign language anyway?

Are you just not feeling the motivation to learn your new language anymore?

Well, the reality is you can't learn very well if you don't understand WHY you're doing it.

Learning a new language is a daunting task that requires strong personal motivation. The more compelling your reason WHY, the more likely you are to succeed. Some of the advantages of learning a new language will be discussed later here in our book. You may or may not be able to use any of these reasons, but the purpose of this list is just to provide you with some ideas to help you come up with your own personal list of WHY's.

Developing Your Cognitive Skills and Strengthening Your Brain.

The ability to recall information and make sound judgments has been demonstrated to increase when you learn a new language. Even Alzheimer's may be delayed by becoming a bilingual or a multilingual person, according to peer-reviewed research. Keeping your brain in shape is a lot like exercising any other muscle in your body. New language acquisition is like a physical challenge but for the mind. It's a great way to keep your brain running at its peak efficiency. This means that you'll be exposed to a wide range of new vocabulary in the process of connecting with locals and native speakers over time, as well as learning to identify and reproduce new sounds in the process. In addition to improving your memory, this brain training may help you learn new talents in the future, as well.

Personal development and growth.

As with any trip, one's personal development occurs along the way while learning a new language. It doesn't matter whether your aim is to learn a new language, get your black belt in kung fu, or start your own company; you'll become a better, stronger, and more competent person as you move forward through your journey. When learning a new language, the borders of your comfort zone will be pushed to the limit.

At times it can be nerve-wracking to have to communicate with someone in a language you don't know well. It's a wonderful feeling to get over your fear of public speaking and realize that you don't have to be flawless to communicate. You will become a more FEARLESS person as a result of this process. All of the little triumphs along the way will give you a tremendous feeling of accomplishment.

Increased Marketability.

You'll have a better shot at getting a job if you can speak another language. This is a highly sought-after ability in almost every industry. Even if the languages spoken aren't necessary for the job, employers value bilingual skills as an indicator of competence and intellect. On your resume or CV, it's always a good thing to have. When you learn a new language, you open up a whole new world of possibilities. You will be able to communicate with your clients and customers in their native language, which will help you build a stronger, more memorable, and more lasting connection with them. Even your colleagues may start referring business to you. For the most part, this is beneficial, and it may help you acquire and retain a higher-paying job, depending on the sort of work you do.

Educate Yourself on Other People's Culture.

When you learn a new language, you will naturally come to know more than just the language. It will broaden your horizons and alter your outlook on life. You'll meet fascinating folks from all walks of life. Traveling will be a lot more pleasant, comfortable, and less stressful if you learn the language of the people. Even though English is widely spoken in popular tourist destinations across the world, becoming fluent in the local language will provide you the freedom to explore places off the beaten path, less frequented by tourists.

It is not necessary to go far from the central tourist locations to discover that not everyone can communicate well in English. Having the ability to converse with locals in their own language really transforms the experience of your trip. As a result, you may find yourself eating supper with a local family. Lifting your head up from all the delicious food before your eyes, you look around, and a beautiful opportunity emerges, a precious moment is yours to make meaningful connections with people who practice a way of life that is very different from your own. Through these unexpected encounters, you can get a new elevated perspective on the world and learn about its fascinating cultural variety. With all of this additional experience, you'll have the opportunity to enjoy the original quality of your favorite works of art and entertainment without having to worry about them being corrupted throughout the translation process.

"BUT I STILL CAN'T UNDERSTAND THE NATIVE SPEAKERS!"

Learners of a new language often find it difficult to understand native speakers. It's one of the most common roadblocks that adults face while learning a new language. Somewhere down the line, after believing yourself to be well on your way to mastering a foreign language, you might hear someone speak and find yourself completely baffled, wondering "Why don't I know this already?" For most people, it's hard to accept this, but it's essential to your progress to keep moving forward when these types of feelings crop up. You may not be as far off from fluency as you think. It can be hard to comprehend native speakers for a variety of reasons. A few recommendations on how to enhance your progress toward fluency are included in this chapter, which examines the numerous causes of a learner's lack of comprehension.

• There is an absence of comprehensive holistic knowledge.

Because some learners are not familiar with enough vocabulary, they may not be able to comprehend native speakers as fast as they would like to. You would think that this might be more apparent, but the contrast between almost understanding the words uttered and having no idea what they mean is crucial. Sometimes it's difficult to tell whether you didn't comprehend anything because it was spoken too fast or if you just didn't grasp the words due to a local accent or regional dialect.

Think about how you would've said it... When pronouncing the words yourself, do you notice your breathing, cadence, position of your lips, and how much air you are using to speak your language out loud? Ask yourself: Would it have made any difference if I spoke more slowly or used less air to say the phrase correctly? Can you think of any other interesting ways to get a better sense of your overall abilities?

• Transcribing a Movie: Putting Your Skills to the Test.

If you're watching a movie or TV show in a foreign language and you don't understand much, consider turning on the dubbing feature in your target language, and the subtitles in English to help you. How much better can you follow along with what is being said if you can follow along with what is being read? To watch a program without subtitles the viewer has to acquire a lot more vocabulary before they can grasp what is happening.

• Listening to a language with a higher vocabulary.

Listening to natural fluent speech requires a larger vocabulary than reading. To gain an overall sense of the material in printed form, you may only need to comprehend a lower percentage of the words you read since a person can frequently deduce and even learn a few terms from context. For conversations with native speakers, though, it's a whole other ballgame altogether. There is just so much to take in at the beginning, so take it slow, there's no rush. Remember, your brain learns better & soaks in more information in a relaxed state. That's why comprehending things that are written down differs so much from understanding spoken language.

- It is common for native speakers to mumble and speak at a rapid pace.

As your language skills improve, you'll be able to comprehend more of what you read, but you may still find it difficult to communicate with people who are native speakers. No worries, this is normal and for some, it may be a difficult part of the process of learning a new language. Because they are so familiar with their own language, native speakers can have a tendency to make careless mistakes, such as mumbling, or skipping whole words, phrases, or syllables. All of us do it, and it's a natural part of the way we communicate in every language. Even if you don't know all the words you hear, it's not that difficult to get your brain acclimated to hearing them rapidly and learning common acronyms and contractions that people from other countries use.

- The more foreign material you hear, the better it'll be.

At any level, it is usually advisable to immerse yourself in the language by listening to it as often as possible. When done correctly, your brain will do the heavy lifting for you and you will progressively become more comfortable with unfamiliar noises, breathing, and speech patterns using this method. Simply choose a resource or type of media that touches your heart, closely connects with YOUR WHY and that is appropriate for your current level of expertise. A good place to begin could be with material geared towards youngsters under the age of two. After that, you may check out movies for the whole family, such as those from Disney or DreamWorks. Movies you've SEEN BEFORE may also be listened to in dubbed format from these sources. Slowly move up to viewing movies filmed in your target language, after you've mastered the other films you have seen previously in English. As you proceed up the difficulty scale, you will be less likely to feel overwhelmed, and it will be simpler to keep track of your progress. This gradual increase in difficulty is critical since it serves as a far better motivator than attempting to dive immediately into more difficult content.

- Hearing a totally different tone of speech.

This is for those who have a firm grasp of the material. When you've mastered a new language, you'll come across content or individuals who you can't comprehend at all! This often occurs as a result of the speaker's unique accent or dialect. Even in your native tongue, this may happen. If an American English speaker visits a Scottish hamlet in the middle of nowhere, they may have a difficult time comprehending the language of the local people, even though they both speak English... LOL.

The context in which a language is spoken may also have an effect on how it is perceived. In other words, if you're used to watching medical documentaries on TV and then switching to watching a romantic comedy, the characters' speech patterns may be very different. After a certain degree of proficiency though it's typically effortless to adapt to a new language's idioms & unique phrases. You'll gradually grow acclimated to the new noises if you just keep listening and keeping your ears open to them. To consolidate a bit here, one of the fastest methods children use to become fluent in their language lightning-fast is to immerse themselves in it as much as possible. As adults, we can copy their techniques by keeping our ears on, when we find native speakers around us.

"OKAY, BUT THIS IS HARD'

Although the most difficult component of learning a new language differs for each person, there are six common difficulties that seem to be encountered by the majority of learners. I want to meet you in the middle and go through some of the difficulties you may encounter, and provide some helpful guidance on how to overcome them.

Just getting started!

In general, the most difficult aspect of learning a new language is the beginning for many people. mostly because they have no idea where to begin. Do you begin with the basics of grammar? Do you begin by memorizing essential phrases or should you start the process with flashcards and phonics drills? For some, the adventure has ended before it's even begun because of all the questions they have to answer. This isn't how it has to be. It is important to keep in mind that no matter what route you choose on your language journey, you will always find success when you KEEP MOVING FORWARD.

If you're just starting out, having a strategy might make the experience more pleasurable. It's up to you to choose a resource that works best for your learning style and wallet. A high-quality language course like a FLUENZ Language Immersion might be a good option for those who want to learn a new language. Learning on your own becomes much simpler if you have a good foundation.

- Learning How To Approach Thousands of New Phrases and Word Origins.

There are lots of words in a language. But all of them are not necessarily the most important words to learn at the outset. You will however, ultimately need to know hundreds if not thousands of them. Most individuals may find this daunting, and it may even seem impossible at first. Until you discover all the secret weapons in this book. 📘

No matter how many new words you pick up along the way, it doesn't take much effort to become fluent in using them all. Remember that even little measures may make a big difference in the long run of your journey.

What do you think? How many words do you believe you can recite in Spanish today? And, what about the next day? And next week? A year from now, you'll have learned more than 1,000+ words if you learn only three words a day. A more manageable task becomes apparent when you break down your overall goal into smaller, more manageable components.

When learning a new language, one of the most frequent problems students run into is forgetting the words they've previously learned. It's a never-ending cycle of education when this happens. How can you ensure that you remember what you've learned over time?

There are several ways to describe the memory boosting super-powers of your brain 🧠. We will discuss a few more later in the book. Without oversimplifying them, these are some of the same

"Golden Keys 🔑" that have already unlocked YOUR BRAIN'S learning potential as a kid!

A few of them are:

Physical movement during learning, novelty for your brain, "show & tell" by teaching others, using "hooks" with your 5-Senses and repetition for reinforcement. It's imperative that you immerse yourself in the language as much as possible. Trying to recall words if you don't hear or use them again is difficult. After learning the words, immerse yourself in the environment where people use your target language daily, and you'll find that remembering the words isn't nearly as difficult as it seems. In fact, it will become quite intuitive, instinctively fluent & commonplace for your brain.

- Actually going out to meet native speakers.

Not everybody has a Japanese friend, and even if you did, they may not be willing to risk a beautiful relationship with you for becoming your language teacher. LOL… And then when you finally get a native speaker in your same classroom at school, at your office, or maybe living next door, they end up talking so fast, you're just ready to give up in a few seconds!

In the past, we've all heard that native speakers talk a little too quickly. Across the board, this is true for every language. They can understand each other even if they slur their way through the statement since, of course, they are native speakers. Listening to the language as much as possible is the best treatment, once again. Remember to look at the native speaker's mouth as it moves. Notice their breathing patterns, and when they take a breath during their sentence. Listen to audiobooks, podcasts, and other media.

Keep in mind that it's preferable to start with content that isn't too complex for you and work your way up gradually. As a beginner, you should mix in content that's geared for kids, then work your way up the difficulty scale as you go along. Proceed with caution, because if not approached with this hybrid way of learning, it may be difficult, if not impossible when you are unable to comprehend what is being said later. With some perseverance and a few words of wisdom, though, you can make some headway. If you listen to a lot of different kinds of material, your listening skills will develop nicely.

- Having conversations with completely unrelated influences.

Everyone has unique circumstances and unique desires. But in our experience, our client's ultimate desire is to have an authentic conversation with someone in their mother tongue, to genuinely communicate with another person. Language learners can often allow themselves to be paralyzed by the fear of seeming foolish or making errors. As a result, how can we overcome this anxiety about communicating in another language? (psst... Remember, KIDS are not scared to make mistakes... So just copy them)

Fortunately, there are techniques to lessen this dreadful sensation. Reach out for help from someone who is patient and understands what it is like to learn a new language from the beginning. On the internet, you'll discover individuals who consistently engage in conversations with language learners. People currently around you that are familiar with your face, at your local grocery store, local library, local hotel catering to people of your target language group, and even your local Assisted Living Facility for the elderly or Center for Retirees can be of great help to you.. They can help make you feel more comfortable as you work on your skills in a safe & encouraging environment. No matter how nervous you are, you must push through it. After all is said and done, it's an exhilarating sensation. After a few chats like this with your people, your self-esteem will soar, and the uneasiness will subside almost immediately.

"HOW LONG IS THIS GOING TO TAKE, ANYWAY?"

Oh, I get that a lot. More times than I can count. And my response never changes.

"That depends on the person."

Of course, my students poke and prod for a better answer that never actually happens.

We live in a society today that needs a definitive answer immediately. We need to know how long something will take so we can plan accordingly.

How long does it take? How much time? These are the kinds of questions they're seeking answers to. That's only the beginning. There's more to it than that. When it comes to learning a new language, and you're feeling a little antsy about time, take a look at this checklist to help cool your nerves.

I say it is not so much about time, but more about EFFORT. It's kind of like farming... If you only plant one seed per day. How much fruit do you think you will harvest at the end of the season? But if you plant many seeds each day... Tell me how much fruit will be popping off your trees at harvest time? Think about fluently speaking your language in the same way.

- Transform your mental condition.

When learning a language, it's better not to focus on a set timeline. Sadly, most learners with this perspective will find it very difficult to become fluent in the language. The issue is that as time passes they become more concerned with the final destination than the process of getting there. While you may be able to talk fluently in a matter of months, you will continue to learn throughout your life. For the rest of your life, practicing will make you a little bit better each week.

- The process of picking up a new language is one that happens over time.

Practicing your language is a great way to improve your skills over time. The good news is that you'll make the most significant progress in the beginning. When things begin to slow down, it doesn't mean you're not making progress; your progress may simply be less obvious momentarily. Even in your native tongue, you're probably still picking up a few new words & phrases every now and again. In addition, your proficiency in your home language is the result of many hours spent practicing it. You wouldn't be as good if you quit practicing your very first language after you attained "fluency," right?

- Time is relative… Your FLUENCY will be more indicative of EFFORT

One of the most important variables in your capacity to learn and retain new words is your personal ability to acquire and retain new words in a foreign language. In any event, the amount of time spent with the language should be expressed in hours rather than months or years. Hours of exposure to your target language each week. The most important decision is how much time you're willing to devote EACH DAY to the project. A basic level of proficiency in languages like Spanish, French, and Italian may be achieved after roughly 500 hours of study, according to some preliminary estimates.

- Learn to appreciate the journey.

Again, SUCCESS LEAVES CLUES… As adults, we tend to get the best results by returning to what is natural, adopting a childlike approach, using techniques inspired by nature, which we will soon discuss a little further in the book.

Learn to appreciate the little steps you take each day. Finding a technique you love, being consistent, and never giving up are the keys to success for learning a new language. You can achieve fluency and beyond by tapping into your childlike roots back when you learned your very first language. This may also be a major reason why many people look back on their childhood with memories of fun, wonder and a time full of vibrant imagination. If you're able to accomplish that, using these valuable techniques now in adulthood, your journey to fluency will be a rewarding experience that you'll cherish for the rest of your life. Enjoy your journey!

CHAPTER 9
METHODS FOR LIGHTNING-FAST FLUENCY

"If you talk to a man in a language he understands, that goes to his head. If you talk to him in his own language, that goes to his heart."

— NELSON MANDELA

THE PIMSLEUR METHOD

The Pimsleur Method for learning new languages was established by Dr. Paul Pimsleur (1927-1976). Dr. Pimsleur was an accomplished academic who received his Ph.D. from Columbia University. He became a professor at UCLA and Ohio State. Highly respected in his field, the prestigious American Council on Foreign Languages (ACTFL) named an annual award after him: The Paul Pimsleur Award for Research in Foreign Language Education.

Paul Pimsleur's "research focused on understanding the language acquisition process, ESPECIALLY THE LEARNING PROCESS OF CHILDREN, who speak their language without knowing its formal structure. The result of this research was the Pimsleur language learning system." Pimsleur, P. (2013).

I feel that the Pimsleur method for language learning is one of the most convenient methods a person can utilize during their language learning process. Not only does The Pimsleur Method allow learners who are not consistently immersed in their target language to carry around quality, immersive, and engaging language lessons in their back pocket. But it also allows the learner's brain to absorb the information in a more relaxed state, than if the learner were speaking to an actual human in a conversation.

One benefit is that The Pimsleur Method allows the learner to rewind any sections of speech that the learner does not understand or does not hear clearly, even multiple times, thus saving the learner the embarrassment of asking an actual person to repeat themselves. In addition, a benefit of this method is the way in which the new language is encoded into your ready-to-learn brain. The Pimsleur Method reverse engineers sentences and phrases in your target language. Resulting in the language learner achieving an enhanced ability to recall & remember their new target language more easily.

Boosting the memory power of the learner, greatly increases the learner's SELF-CONFIDENCE to master their newly acquired language.

Using the Pimsleur Language Learning System myself, in my own multi-language study and acquisition, has proved to be a wonderful tool! I feel that the Pimsleur Method is great for learning any new language. It's very effective, fun, and empowering for your learning journey.

All in all, The Pimsleur Method for learning a new language is an awesome and fun way to learn how to speak and understand the speech of other people in your new language! Which I might add is a major part, some experts may even say the most valuable part of learning any new language. However, The Pimsleur Method is not totally comprehensive for a student's language acquisition in that it does not assist the student in learning how to write or read in the student's target language.

TOTAL PHYSICAL RESPONSE

Total Physical Response (TPR) is a language teaching & learning method built around the coordination of speech and action together; it attempts to teach language through physical (motor) activity. This method is a great tool to have in your toolbox, because TPR is able to reach you & the person you speak with at their level, no matter which learning style the particular person uses more dominantly, to absorb and retain information. TPR is able to help you to understand & respond in your target language and is able to reach people that are Audial Learners, Visual Learners, and Kinetic or Tactile Learners.

Just as an artist paints their canvas with many different types & sizes of paint brushes, TPR is a very useful tool, possibly even the most used tool, for you to create a language 'masterpiece' and really master your new language.

English Speaking Adults tend to converse with phrases that may not include any gestures. An example may be: "Hey, how's it going today?" The other person may respond by saying: "Pretty good, but I've been having a bit of trouble at the office recently."

However, many times, children tend to express themselves with rich, meaningful "body movements that are automatically synchronized with their language." Leaving behind their adult counterparts, to eat their linguistic dust! As the saying goes, in the field of language learning, "adults have a learning context that is poor as body movements rarely represent a clue to understanding what is said" by other adults.

-Mauro Morretta, Maria Grazia De Francisci (2014)

TPR is absolutely essential for accelerating your learning process for new language acquisition. All students can benefit from this language learning method, and with practice, it should come very naturally to each person reading this book since we have all been using some form of TPR since birth. For adult students though, it may take a little extra practice.

SINGING

Singing is something that comes so naturally to many different lifeforms on our planet. Insects, animals, humans, and even angels ALL sing.

It has been said that our words invoke thought, and our melody invokes feelings, but a SONG, a song can place MY WORDS INTO YOUR HEART... This modern proverb captures the essence of how powerful music & songs can be when helping you acquire a foreign language.

So use this superpower to your advantage!

After reflecting on the subject, knowing that human infants learn to sing before they learn to speak, it will seem to be a reasonable hypothesis that the use of songs and singing have been used by humans to learn and acquire new languages, since the birth of language itself. It is no wonder singing, and the use of song can be such effective & motivating tools to help students learn their target language.

"The purpose of language teaching and learning is defined as developing intercultural communicative competence (cf. Müller-Hartmann, 2009: 18), it is clearly visible that language learning is not only concerned with acquiring knowledge (about grammar and pronunciation systems, for example) - it is not just something we learn about. Rather, it is a skill or a set of skills - something we learn to do. (Gower et al. 1995: 85)" - Richard Grünert (2009)

The student's language skills must be developed in a way that allows them to integrate with the other previously acquired parts of the language. These skills cannot be developed in isolation or independently of each other. This is because most language learning situations involve a mixture of skills that are interrelated together. Thus requiring the Language Coach to help the learner develop these skills with a more holistic mindset.

Music and singing are a part of everyday life and play an important role in the lives of most people. Young people especially love music. In many cases, music in your target language is very easy to find.

Please remember to pay attention to the song choice. Many songs convey a particular message. Learners, young and old, can identify or relate to the content of songs. Especially when the song touches on a topic the person is interested in or is currently experiencing in their life (such as being lovesick or having problems in their social environment). Each one of you, as language learners, can grab this opportunity to make use of the song's lyrics to help further your progress in language acquisition and bind the new words to the EMOTIONS OF YOUR HEART.

Another positive aspect of learning a new language through the use of songs and music is that it provides something different for "study time." It can be viewed as an alternative to the common methods of language learning and can be viewed as a very interactive way of learning from the learner's point of view. This may be due to the intrinsic nature of singing & music's ability not just to speak to the mind but also its ability to SPEAK TO YOUR HEART. Which is something that has been said to transcend language itself… Wow, that was deep. Even for me.

DUOLINGO

Unlock Lightning-Fast Fluency with DuoLingo

Now, let's talk about turbocharging your progress with one of the most popular language-learning apps out there: DuoLingo.

DuoLingo isn't just any language-learning app; it's your ticket to lightning-fast fluency. How? Let me break it down for you.

It's got Bite-Sized Lessons, with Big-Time Results:

DuoLingo's lessons are designed to be short, sweet, and oh-so-effective. Each session is like a power-packed language workout, targeting key skills like vocabulary, grammar, listening, and speaking. By breaking down language learning into manageable chunks, DuoLingo keeps you engaged and motivated, helping you make consistent progress every day. You see, they know how distracting & addictive all the other apps on your device can be. So they took the BEST & MOST engaging aspects of your addictive apps that interfere with your progress and they included them into Duolingo's language learning experience.

Now your brain doesn't have to choose between consuming virtual "cake" and let's say "broccoli" on your smartphone anymore. Now you can have your "cake" and eat it too!... Lol

Gamification for the Win:

Who said learning couldn't be fun? DuoLingo gamifies the language-learning experience, turning each lesson into a playful challenge. Earn points, level up, and unlock rewards as you conquer new words and phrases. It's like leveling up in your favorite video game, except this time, you're leveling up your language skills. Now you're getting a real superpower!

Personalized Learning, Tailored to You:

No two learners are alike, and DuoLingo gets that. That's why it personalizes your learning experience based on your strengths, weaknesses, and goals. Whether you're a total beginner or brushing up on your skills, DuoLingo adapts to your level, ensuring that every lesson is just right for you. Plus, with its intelligent algorithms tracking your progress, you'll always know exactly where you stand on your language-learning journey.

Practice Anytime, Anywhere & On The Go:

With DuoLingo, there are no excuses for slacking off. Got a few minutes to spare while waiting for your morning coffee? Whip out your smartphone and knock out a quick lesson. Stuck in line at the supermarket afterwork? Pop in your headphones and practice your listening skills. DuoLingo gives you the flexibility to practice anytime, anywhere, so you can squeeze in language learning whenever it fits into your busy schedule.

Community Support and Accountability:

Learning a new language can feel like a solo mission at times, but with DuoLingo, you're never alone. Join a vibrant community of language learners from around the world, share your progress, and cheer each other on. Whether you're celebrating a breakthrough or overcoming a challenge, your fellow DuoLingo enthusiasts are there to support you every step of the way. Plus, a little friendly competition never hurts, right?

So, what are you waiting for? Dive into DuoLingo today and unlock the secrets to lightning-fast fluency. With its bite-sized lessons, gamified approach, personalized learning, on-the-go practice, and supportive community, DuoLingo has what you need to become a language-learning legend.

MUSCLE MEMORY

Learning to speak & write a language "is to some extent comparable to learning to play a musical instrument, where the learner is required to execute a certain sequence of movement and thus exercises this sequence over and over. The learner thereby develops an association with muscle memory and eventually has the ability to instinctively perform the process (or instrument playing) in a fluent, spontaneous way."

- Chris Shei, Monica E McLellan Zikpi, Der-Lin Chao

When we are learning a new foreign language, we may encounter some differences from our mother tongue that will even engage different muscles in our body we never knew we had! One example may be, transitioning from a Romanized Language with an alphabet to a character-based language, which uses pictograms & ideograms. For instance, in the Chinese, Japanese or Korean languages, besides the physical element of using different muscles and a different breathing pattern than you are accustomed to in your native tongue, there is also the physical element of writing the language. "The traditional way of learning Chinese characters is also referred to as the 'pen-and-paper approach'... 1. Writing the strokes in the correct direction... 2. Following the stroke order... 3. Writing the complete character repetitively... the three aforementioned steps are essential to guaranteeing the development of so-called MUSCLE MEMORY for writing the pictograms & idiograms that make up characters. Muscle memory is known to help consolidate skill-related memorization involving, for instance, hand movement." Using the Muscle Memory Method in learning to write a character-based language can be VERY EFFECTIVE in establishing the brain-body connection. It can also facilitate the construction of smooth & fluent language.

- Chris Shei, Monica E McLellan Zikpi, Der-Lin Chao (2020)

It should be noted that while the Muscle Memory Method can be an effective way for you to achieve comfort and fluency in your target language, this should not be taken to undermine other active, mindful processes that are essential to processing any new foreign language. These other active, mindful processes provide additional "hooks" for your brain to connect to, which aid in your memorization by asserting logical and/or distinctive cognitive links by which the new target language can be negotiated in your memory.

IDIOMS

Idioms have a special place in my heart. These unique proverbs, I feel, open a large window into THE SOUL OF THE LANGUAGE and the culture of the people who use that language every day! Some idioms are so expressive, that they are figuratively dripping with emotions.

"What is an idiom, and why can they sometimes be so difficult to understand? An idiom can be defined as a phrase which has a different meaning from the meaning of its separate components. One of the characteristics of idioms is that you cannot normally change the words, their order, or the grammatical forms in the same way as you can change non-idiomatic expressions. In other words, idioms are basically fixed expressions."

- Michael P. Berman (2011)

Generally, you will want to have already achieved a certain level of fluency in the language learning process in order to comprehend and properly use the newly acquired idioms that you have just learned.

So you must be in tune with your progress & fluency level to ensure you understand the meaning behind the idiom when others use it, and also the TIMING for when to use the idiom itself.

Sometimes, when people use idioms, the learner can guess the meaning of the idiom by listening to the context of the whole sentence or by examining the meaning of one or more of the words in the idiom itself. But usually, the meaning of the individual words themselves are completely different from the meaning behind the idiom. This is why idioms can be so confusing for language learners. In some instances, it Is necessary for the Language Coach to explain the etymology behind some of the words in the established idiom. This could possibly be due to the time period that the idiom comes from. In English, some idioms have formed from the time when people spoke Middle English. Or what people commonly think of as "Archaic English" or "Old English". Understanding why those particular words are chosen in the idiom, may better help your memorization and comprehension. This takes the idiom from a purely intellectual exercise to now becoming an expression of your heart.

WORD ASSOCIATIONS

New vocabulary is one of the most important things for students learning a second language to acquire. Sadly, many students learning a foreign language are only trying to translate or transliterate words from their mother tongue into the unfamiliar words of their target language or vice versa. Unfortunately, when they do this, they lose the valuable opportunity of associating any mental images of anything to "hook" onto the new vocabulary in their target language.

From birth, when we humans acquire our first spoken language, generally referred to as our native language, we normally do this through word associations. We do this by projecting mental pictures of solid & stable words, as well as abstract words. Through OUR FIVE SENSES, we can associate new vocabulary words that we learn each day. As an example, when we see or hear the word "Hot," we see, smell, and taste such things as a hot stove in the kitchen, hot soup with the steam rising from it, a hot iron ready to press clothes, or even hot peppers that burn in your mouth.

These word associations can help to provide a much more EFFICIENT, DIRECT, and SIMPLE way for you to acquire new vocabulary. It also provides you with more "hooks" helping you to recall the new vocabulary once it's memorized. These hooks that I am referring to establish different pathways in our brains that give us multiple points of access to these new vocabulary words in our target language. All five senses can be viewed as different hooks that can hook into the new vocabulary word. The gift of sight, smell, touch, taste, and hearing can all be used to hook into the same vocabulary word. In my opinion, the more hooks, the better and more efficient your recall of the new vocabulary will be.

Regrettably, many teachers have focused solely on students learning the new vocabulary, rather than examining the way in which this new vocabulary is learned by the student, in the realm of applied neuroscience. Many teachers have approached vocabulary in the same way of "Canale and Swain's seminal paper on communicative competence, which was to define the dominant paradigm in SLA for many years, which had reduced vocabulary knowledge to a very minor role in grammar competence (Canale & Swain 1980). With hindsight, however, it is perhaps more of a surprise that so few people were taking vocabulary acquisition seriously. This, after all, was the heyday of Verbal Learning - a vast area of psychological research, with words, how we learn them and how we use them, and what we can learn about memory and cognition by studying the way people handle words." Paul Meara (2009)

CHAPTER 10

THE FIVE

FLUENTBRAIN HABITS

"Language and identity are so fundamentally intertwined. You peel back all the layers in terms of what we wear and what we eat and all the things that mark us, and in the end, what we have are our words."

— JHUMPA LAHIRI

1. Learn a Word a Day & Engage with Pimsleur:

Ah, simplicity! Dr. Daniel Amen once wisely remarked, "Your brain is involved in everything you do." Thus, enveloping your brain in daily doses of new words and sultry Pimsleur Language Recordings is the quintessential start. Pick an easy, fun word, and let it roll around on your tongue, like tasting a new exotic dish. Lend your ears to the melodious linguistic tunes of Pimsleur Language Recordings for a mere 100 days, where you'll casually pick up the 100 most commonly used words in your new language. Practice it in a sentence, whisper it to your plants, and shout it out-loud during a jog! While traversing through your every day routine, let the melodic tones of your target language weave patterns through your eardrums, seamlessly merging new sounds with everyday activities. Cooking, commuting, or exercising, your new language will weave into every corner of your life.

2. Musical Immersion:

Songs are the heartbeat of a culture, and immersing yourself in at least 2 songs per day is your ticket to linguistic and cultural fluency. It can even be the SAME 2 SONGS all week long if you like... Lol! Just two songs- that's less than 7 minutes of your day spent serenading your brain with melodious vocabulary, accent, and perhaps a catchy dance move or two. Listen, dance, decipher the lyrics, and let the rhythm guide your intonation and pronunciation. Much like Jim Kwik often touts, "Knowledge is not power; it's potential power. Execution is power." So, execute that play button and dive into the melodic charms of your new language!

3. Incorporate Physical Movement While Learning & Curate TV Shows Designed for Young Learners:

Here's a crazy idea: immerse yourself into the world of children, 3-4 times a week. Jumpstart your language journey by embracing the kinetic joy of young learners—mix physical movement with linguistic growth, and witness a brain-boosting explosion! When you integrate physical actions with words, your brain's motor cortex lights up!!! Enhancing memory and understanding. STUDIES & RESEARCH HAVE PROVEN that physical activity can improve cognitive function and facilitate the neural connections needed for language acquisition (Dr. Ratey, J., 2008; "Spark: The Revolutionary New Science of Exercise and the Brain").

Spending time with kids or indulging in their TV shows not only enhances your vocabulary with simple, day-to-day words but also ensures a gleeful learning experience. Kids speak pure, unadulterated language, free from the complex jargon we adults just love to confuse ourselves with. They also have no fear of making mistakes, or how others view them. Children are just "FEARLESS"!

4. Coffee and Cooking with Coach:

Imagine the aroma of freshly brewed coffee mingling with the vivacious chatter in your new language surrounding you. At the next table over, you & your Coach hear something like... ("Ni de KaFei hao ma? Mmm, zhe bei KaFei he hao"... Then at the next table you hear... "Este Café es muy bueno! Verdad?"...) Later in the week, see yourself roaming through local markets with your

Language Coach, chatting with native speakers, and navigating through exotic ingredients - your taste buds and your language neurons will thank you. The conversations, the haggling, the playful banter - all while sipping a cup of the local brew and on another occasion, whipping up a cultural culinary masterpiece. It's an immersive experience that is bound to leave a (delicious) lasting impression on your linguistic journey.

5. Show, Tell, Volunteer & Vibe with the Locals:

Have you ever wondered why kids get so excited about Show & Tell at school? Well, there is a hidden genius behind why it works so well and why Teachers love to use it during class time. The build-up to know what will be revealed, what juicy secrets are lurking behind the Teacher's Desk and everyone knows how COOL you will look in front of the whole class when you finally have a "One Up" on all the popular kids in class, because now for a few short moments you get to become the teacher, bringing enlightenment & wisdom to all that adore you, laying gifts of gratitude before your feet... As you teach them about how your cool talking teddy bear is able to read them a bedtime story... LOL But seriously, taking the center of attention, while still a learner, for those few brief moments also allows your brain to whip up some pretty powerful tools & functionality that propels you forward towards fluency on your language journey as well.

Dive into the deep end of linguistic and cultural immersion by volunteering once a week. Choose a cause that makes your heart flutter and delve into a world where every conversation is imbued with genuine emotions, both giving & receiving, a plethora of real-world vocabulary and you'll be soaking up the language organically in no time. Native speakers, authentic interactions, and perhaps even the opportunity to truly make a difference in someone's life - this is where your language learning journey becomes larger than just yourself. Trust us, the returns - linguistic and emotional - are immeasurable.

Remember:

Each one of you will have a unique journey, sprinkled with mispronunciations, mixed-up verbs, giggles, and aha moments! But remember, as you navigate through these "parts unknown", every word, every strange-sounding word, every joyful interaction is crafting a version of you that speaks more than just words - you'll become fluent in "making connections." 🩶

And as you turn this page, envision yourself turning a new leaf in your language adventure. Emerge, with your brain buzzing with new words, a heart open to new tales, and a spirit ready to communicate in hues previously unknown to you.

I believe in you, my friend! YOU got this!

Yours is a future where your words weave bonds across borders, and your tales echo in numerous tongues. Welcome to your next polyglot journey. Welcome to a world crafted uniquely by you!

Your Next Adventure Awaits...

You can slide into our online community at *FluentBrain.Community*, where fellow language enthusiasts are waiting to share tales and tips with you. Subscribe to our newsletter and immerse yourself in a realm where language isn't just spoken; it's alive, thriving, and loved by all. Book your discovery call with us to carve a unique path designed just for you, guiding your steps into a world where every conversation is a new adventure!

So, "Excelsior!", onwards and upwards! To a future where your words weave bonds across borders, and your tales echo in numerous tongues as you travel. Welcome to the next level of your journey.

WORD-A-DAY WONDER-HACKS

A Word a Day & The Pimsleur Prowess

Imagine, in 100 days, you're gracefully painting images through your new language. Each word you select per day acts as a brushstroke, adorning your verbal canvas. Take "Bonjour" for instance. It's not just "Good Morning"; it's a sunlit handshake, an initial smile on a Parisian street. Pimsleur becomes your trustworthy guide, steering you to linguistically and culturally sound destinations.

Delve Deeper: Dive into the etymology of select words, intertwining cultural tales that emanate from them. E.g., "Bonjour" isn't mere politeness; it's a manifestation of France's value on cordiality. On Pimsleur, explore its interval recall theory, acting as a temporal paintbrush, masterfully shaping your memory's canvas by strategically revisiting learned words/phrases, ensuring they don't fade into oblivial wisps.

1, 2, 3... Sprinkle Some Word-a-Day on Your Brain!

First, let's talk about how monumental it can be to learn *just one* new word every day. It's like collecting tiny linguistic treasures – shiny, precious, and oh-so-invaluable! (Shh... Don't tell your brain, but you'll probably retain & recall a lot more than just one word)

Think of your brain as a fancy, elite club – The 'Cerebral Soiree', if you will. Every day, you allow a new word to enter this exclusive party. And guess what? By day 100, you'll have a high energy party of the 100 most VIP words from your target language! They'll be mingling, mixing, and making merry inside your brain. And since they're the cream of the crop, these words are the ones most frequently used by newspapers, TV shows and the people around you. Sneaky and efficient, right?

Pimsleur Is Now The Cool DJ to Your Language Party

Now, imagine that your 'Cerebral Soiree' has some mood music. Enter Pimsleur Language recordings. Think of Pimsleur as that cool, hype DJ that knows just how to get the crowd vibing. Pimsleur doesn't just help you with vocabulary; it gives your new words context, rhythm, and most importantly, life. And the beauty is, you don't have to set aside any "learning time." No siree! Driving to work? Pimsleur's riding shotgun. On the metro, squeezed between two folks debating the merits of pineapple on pizza? Pimsleur's got your back. Doing your laundry, waiting for the spin cycle to finish? That's right, it's Pimsleur o'clock!

The sheer brilliance of this approach is that it's seamless. In no time, you're not just hearing words anymore; you're *living* them. That word you learned in the morning could pop up in your Pimsleur session while you're driving back from work. The universe has a way of sending signs, and sometimes, look out, they're in a foreign tongue!

Why the 100-Day Challenge is a Game-Changer

Now, why, you might wonder, is there all this hullabaloo about 100 days? Why not 50, or 60 or, heck, even 70? Well, my friend, 100 days is that *sweet spot*. It's long enough to help you form a solid habit but short enough to not feel daunting. It's like linguistic Goldilocks territory. Not too long, not too short – it's just right!

A hundred days of consciously learning the most commonly used words in your target language means that you're not just cramming vocabulary – you're immersing yourself in your target language's very culture, rhythm, and soul. By the end of these hundred days, you'll find those words have become your secret weapons to understanding your world around you. They'll pop up in conversations, on street signs, in that Spanish song that's been stuck in your head. Before you know it, these words are comfortably nestled in your daily life, becoming as essential as your morning cuppa joe!

The Genius Behind One-Word-a-Day

You might ask, "Why just one word? Ah, young Padawan, this is the way! One word a day ensures you're not overwhelmed. It's manageable, memorable, and oh-so-doable. It's like getting to know just one new person at school, during your lunch break, rather than trying to befriend an entire football team at once!

Each word gets its day in the sun, its moment of fame in your brain. You get to roll it around in your mind, play with it, use it in sentences, and truly understand its essence.

Bringing It All Together: Words and Rhythms

So, as you dive into your linguistic journey, remember the power of simplicity. Let that one word shine daily. And as it shines, let the rhythms of Pimsleur infuse it with context and life. Before you know it, you're not just learning a language; you're living it.

Together, with me as your guide,, your 100-day challenge awaits. Let's raise a metaphorical glass to the next 100 days of your adventure. And cheers to becoming fantastically fluent!

LANGUAGE THROUGH LYRICS

Tune into the Linguistic Rhythm of Your Heart

Inhabiting the lyrical realm of your chosen language, each new song becomes a journey through emotional and cultural landscapes. For instance, the Italian "Nel Blu, Dipinto Di Blu" (Volare) extends beyond melody; it's a vocalization of Italy's post-war dreams and optimism.

Delve Deeper: Investigate lyrics, reflecting on metaphorical, historical, and emotional significance. Volare, though seemingly a romantic serenade, could represent Italy's soaring hopes during its economic boom. Engage yourself in an active listening strategy: first listen, then dissect, and finally, sing along, ensuring each word leaves a melodic imprint on your linguistic memory.

Turning up the Volume on Language Learning: Two Tunes a Day to Keep the Language Fumbles Away!

Alright, business people, multicultural family members, world travelers, and aspiring polyglots, if you're done stretching those linguistic muscles with the power of one word a day (congrats to you, by the way!), it's time to jam with another "kid-genius" strategy. The dance floor is ready, and YOU will be the DJ this time – MUSIC is the diverse juggernaut of the linguistic world – I know you're gonna spin some killer tracks.

Why Songs?

First, let's talk about why we're using music as our magic carpet ride into the world of language. Remember that one song from your childhood? Yeah, the one that you haven't listened to in years but somehow managed to recite word-for-word during a random karaoke night (while also busting out your impressive, slightly rusty, moonwalk)? That's the power of music!

Songs, with their catchy tunes and rhythmic beats, have this almost otherworldly ability to cement themselves into our memories. Add language learning to that mix, and voilà, you've got yourself an unbeatable combination.

The Power of Dos (That's 'Two' for our Spanish amigos out there!)

While we're all about immersion here, we also want to ensure that you don't end up with linguistic indigestion. You see, by narrowing it down to two songs, you give yourself ample time to really dive deep. You're not just skimming the surface; you're diving deep into the musical abyss, savoring each note, and wrapping your mind around each lyric. Think of it as fine dining, but for your ears!

A Two-Song Strategy to Sway and Slay!

1. **Choose the Right Groove:** While any song can technically teach you something, try aiming for those with clear lyrics. We all love a good fast-paced reggaeton or rapid-fire rap, but when you're starting, clarity is key. Maybe save those tongue twisters for when you're a tad more fluent.
2. **Listen and Jot:** The first time around, just listen to the music. Feel the rhythm, sway to the beat. The second time, have a notepad ready. Jot down words or phrases that jump out at you – kinda like a musical scavenger hunt!
3. **Dive into the Lyrics:** Post jamming, look up the song lyrics. See the words you recognized and those you didn't. Now, here's where the magic happens: translate them. Not just the standalone words, but the context, the idioms, the colloquialisms. Before you know it, you're not just grooving to a beat, you're decoding YOUR new culture.

4. **Sing Along:** This isn't just fun (though, who doesn't love a good sing-along session?), it's also immensely practical. Singing along can significantly improve your pronunciation and fluency. Plus, it's a fantastic stress-buster! Think of it as karaoke, but with benefits.

5. **Rinse and Repeat:** Now, while our strategy is built around two songs, don't feel restricted. If you stumble upon an artist or a genre that resonates with you, by all means, go on a musical binge! The more, the merrier.

The Unexpected Bonuses of the Two-Tune Technique 🎁

- **Cultural Deep Dive:** Songs often reflect the emotions, sentiments, and zeitgeist of a place. By tuning into songs from your target language, you're not just learning words; you're immersing yourself in the very soul of the culture.
- **Ear Training:** Over time, your ears will get attuned to the nuances of the language – the unique intonations, the unique accents, the quirky slang.
- **Conversation Starters:** Next time you meet a native speaker, instead of the clichéd "How's the weather?", you can chat about popular songs or artists. It's a fantastic way to bond and flaunt your impressive (and growing) linguistic prowess.

Wrapping Up with a Musical Bow 🎀

Incorporating music into your language learning journey is like adding a dash of zesty salsa to a bowl of chips. It's flavorful, fun, and oh-so-addictive. Before you know it, you'll be humming tunes in your target language, impressing friends with your amazing karaoke skills, and most importantly, soaking in the language in the most enjoyable way possible.

Now that you're a polyglot in training, embarking on this harmonious journey, remember – two songs a day keep the language blues away! Pop in those earbuds, crank up the volume, and let the music whisk you away to linguistic paradise.

MOVEMENT FOR ADULT BRAINS IS CHILD'S PLAY

It's All Connected (Literally...Lol)

Let's dive into the fascinating world of brain-friendly language learning and how our motor cortex plays a crucial role in the process.

Imagine this: when we move our bodies, whether it's walking, dancing, or even just tapping our fingers, our motor cortex lights up like a Christmas tree.

Now, you might be wondering, "What does that have to do with language learning?" Well, let me tell you.

Research published in peer-reviewed journals like the Journal of Cognitive Neuroscience and Frontiers in Psychology has shown that physical movement is closely linked to cognitive function, including language processing. When we engage in activities that involve movement, we activate various regions of the brain, including those responsible for language acquisition.

For children, this connection is particularly strong. Studies conducted by researchers such as Dr. Laura Batterink at the University of California, Berkeley, have demonstrated that children who engage in physical activities while learning new words show improved retention and recall compared to those who learn in a sedentary environment.

But here's the really cool part: the benefits of movement-based learning aren't limited to kids. Research by Dr. Lara Boyd at the University of British Columbia has shown that adults can also harness the power of physical activity to enhance their language learning abilities.

So, what kinds of movements are we talking about here? It could be anything from walking while practicing vocabulary to acting out scenarios to reinforce grammar concepts. The key is to get your body involved in the learning process.

How to Incorporate Physical Movement with Language Learning for Adults

Incorporating physical movement into your language learning routine isn't just about breaking up the monotony; it's about leveraging the science behind brain function to enhance your acquisition of a new language. Integrating physical activity with language practice can help improve memory retention, increase cognitive flexibility, and make learning more enjoyable. Whether you're hitting the gym or just stretching in your living room, combining movement with language practice can work wonders for your brain. Here's how you can integrate some action into your language routine, igniting your sessions to become dynamic, engaging, and so much more effective.

1. Active Study Sessions

Incorporate Movement into Your Study Routine: Instead of sitting stationary during study sessions, add physical activity to your routine.

Here are some effective methods:

- **Walking While Reviewing:** Grab your headphones and take your language lessons on the go. Whether you're strolling through your neighborhood or hitting the treadmill, listening to language recordings while walking helps boost your brainpower and creativity (Oppezzo & Schwartz, 2014). Just imagine, your daily walk could turn into a mini-language immersion session!
- **Standing Desk:** Use a standing desk while engaging in language study. Standing and moving slightly, like shifting weight or pacing, can increase energy and focus (Morris et al., 2011).

Reference:

- Oppezzo, M., & Schwartz, D. L. (2014). Give your ideas some legs: The positive effect of walking on creative thinking. *Journal of Experimental Psychology: Learning, Memory, and Cognition*, 40(4), 1142-1150. doi:10.1037/a0036577
- Morris, J. A., & Hamer, M. (2011). Physical activity and the brain: What we know. *Journal of Clinical Neurology*, 7(4), 189-196. doi:10.3988/jcn.2011.7.4.189

2. Interactive Learning Activities

Combine Movement with Language Practice Out-Loud: Engage in activities that combine physical movement with language learning tasks:

- **Flashcard Frenzy:** Scatter flashcards around your room or backyard. As you move from card to card, practice the words and phrases. This active approach not only makes learning more physical but also helps reinforce memory through movement (Klein, 2007).

- **Language Learning Games:** Participate in physical language games such as charades or Pictionary with a language-learning twist. For example, act out new vocabulary words or phrases and have others guess them. This method taps into both visual and kinetic learning styles (Gardner, 2006).

Reference:

- Klein, P. D. (2007). A developmental perspective on the role of movement in learning. *Educational Psychology Review*, 19(3), 227-247. doi:10.1007/s10648-007-9055-8
- Gardner, H. (2006). Multiple Intelligences: New Horizons in Theory and Practice. *Basic Books*.

3. Incorporate Movement into Language Immersion

Use Movement in Real-Life Language Practice: Integrate movement into everyday language practice by incorporating it your "Native" immersion experiences:

- **Language Walks:** Practice your new language while taking a walk in a local park or at your neighborhood supermarket designed for a cultural & ethnic experience. Engage with native speakers or listen to audio recordings in your target language as you walk around (Colcombe & Kramer, 2003).
- **Exercise Classes:** Join exercise classes conducted in your target language. This combines physical activity with language immersion and provides an opportunity to learn

new vocabulary related to fitness and exercise (Kramer et al., 2006).

Reference:

- Colombe, S. J., & Kramer, A. F. (2003). Fitness effects on the cognitive function of older adults: A meta-analytic study. *Psychological Science*, 14(2), 125-130. doi:10.1111/1467-9280.t01-1-01430
- Kramer, A. F., & Erickson, K. I. (2006). Effects of physical activity on cognition and brain function. *Neuropsychology*, Development, and Cognition. Section B, Aging, Neuropsychology and Cognition, 13(3), 234-239. doi:10.1080/13825580500280595

4. Create a Routine with Regular Physical Activity

Consistency is Key: Make physical activity a regular part of your learning routine:

- **Daily Movement:** Incorporate a 30-minute exercise session into your daily routine. Pair it with language practice by listening to language podcasts or reviewing vocabulary. It's like killing two birds with one stone—staying fit and learning a new language (Ratey, 2008).
- **Use Active Brain Breaks:** Use physical movement as a study break. For example, after studying for 25-30 minutes, take a 5-10 minute break to do some light stretching or a quick workout. This can help refresh your mind and enhance learning efficiency (Tomporowski, 2003).

Reference:

- Ratey, J. J. (2008). Spark: The Revolutionary New Science of Exercise and the Brain. *Little, Brown and Company.*
- Tomporowski, P. D. (2003). Effects of acute bouts of exercise on cognition. *Acta Psychologica,* 112(3), 297-324. doi:10.1016/S0001-6918(02)00134-8

5. Engage in Social Physical Activities

Combine Social Interaction with Physical Movement:

Engage in group activities that combine language practice with physical movement:

- **Language Learning Groups:** Join or form a language learning group that meets in person and incorporates physical activities such as hiking or sports. Social interaction and movement together can make learning more motivating and enjoyable (Bailey, 2001).
- **Active Language Games:** Participate in group games that require physical activity and language use, such as scavenger hunts or role-playing scenarios in your target language. It's a fun way to learn while staying active (Vygotsky, 1978).

Reference:

- Bailey, K. M. (2001). Language teaching research and language pedagogy. *Wiley-Blackwell.*
- Vygotsky, L. S. (1978). Mind in Society: The Development of Higher Psychological Processes. *Harvard University Press.*

By incorporating these methods into your language learning routine, you leverage the power of physical movement to boost your cognitive function and enhance your overall learning experience. So, lace up those sneakers, get moving, and let your language-learning journey be both active and effective! The key is to make the integration of movement enjoyable and consistent, ensuring that it complements and enriches your language acquisition journey.

Think about it like this: when you move your body, you're not just engaging your muscles; you're also stimulating your brain. And when it comes to language learning, the more parts of your brain you can activate, the better.

So, the next time you're studying a new language, don't be afraid to get up and get moving. Whether you're practicing yoga poses while reciting vocabulary or dancing to foreign-language music, remember that every little movement is helping to strengthen those neural connections in your brain.

CHILDREN & CARTOONS: YOUR UNEXPECTED LANGUAGE GURUS

Alright, all you brave souls out there who have journeyed this far with me into our book, are you ready to embark on the next wild chapter of your language-learning odyssey? Fasten your seat belts & sippy cups and make sure your tray tables are in their full upright position. (just a heads-up) We're diving headfirst into the realm of... kiddos and cartoons!

Why Kids, Though?

I see you there, squinting skeptically at these words. Stick with me for a sec. Have you ever noticed how kids just seem to soak up languages like adorable little sponges? They don't care about conjugations, verb tables, or grammatical gender. They just... speak. They try, they err, they get up, and they go again. Kids are linguistic rockstars, minus the diva tantrums (well, most of the time).

Here's why hanging with the young'uns can supercharge your language acquisition:

- **Simple Vocabulary:** Little Timmy isn't going to chat about existential dread or discuss the economic implications of global trade. He's more likely to tell you about his toy car or the big dog he saw. That's the beauty of it. Kids use straightforward, everyday words, making it easier for you to pick up and understand.
- **Repetition, Repetition, Repetition:** Have you ever heard a kid tell a story? They'll repeat the same phrase or sentence multiple times. This might seem monotonous, but for a language learner? It's pure gold. Repetition is key to retention.
- **They're Forgiving:** Mistake in front of a kiddo? They won't judge. They might giggle, or they might just continue chatting about their day. It's a judgment-free zone.

Get Moving, Get Learning

Step into the vibrant dance of words and movement, where each step, each sway, each playful jump is a leap towards MASTERING YOUR NEW LANGUAGE. Imagine this: you're not just sitting passively watching "Peppa Pig" in Spanish; you're actively mimicking the characters' actions, engaging your entire body in the language learning process. Movement isn't just good for your muscles—it's a potent catalyst for your brain!

Why Combine Movement with Language Learning?

Here's the real genius hiding in plain sight: Engaging in physical activity while learning not only keeps your energy levels up but also enhances your brain's ability to remember new information. According to a study published in the "Journal of Cognitive Neuroscience," physical activity increases the brain's plasticity, making it more receptive to new information and better at retaining it. This is due to the stimulation of the motor cortex, which is involved both in planning and executing movement and in processing new linguistic structures for children and adults alike.

Delve Deeper: Write down and schedule into your day actionable steps for infusing childlike wonder into your learning: turning everyday routine into play, errors morph into explorative lessons, and seeing every new phrase as a curious puzzle. Reference studies & research (like Vygotsky's Zone of Proximal Development) that highlight the benefits of learning within an 'enjoyable challenge' realm, just as kids do naturally.

The Magic Trio: Movement, Kids' TV, and Language Learning

So, how do we harness this powerful trio? Simple! Combine watching children's TV shows in your target language with physical movement. Before you start, make sure to obtain permission from a parent or legal guardian if you plan to involve children other than your own in these activities. Here's your step-by-step guide:

1. **Choose the Right Show:** Pick a lively children's program in your target language. The show should include plenty of action words and movements that you can mimic.
2. **Mimic and Move:** As you watch, stand up and mimic the movements you see on screen. If a character jumps, you jump. If they dance, you dance. This active participation helps anchor new words and phrases to physical actions, enhancing memory.
3. **Interactive Viewing Sessions:** Don't just watch—interact! Pause the show occasionally to repeat phrases or discuss what happened using the new language. These pauses allow you to process and practice the language actively.
4. **Consistency is Key:** Engage with your chosen TV show three times a week. This frequency ensures that your brain frequently revisits and practices the new language, optimal for building fluency without overwhelming you.
5. **Stay Safe and Respectful:** Always remember, when involving children, whether observing their interactions or participating in activities together, it is essential to have the consent of their parent or legal guardian.

Why Three Times a Week?

Consistency builds habits, and habits build fluency. Immersing yourself in a physically active language learning session three times a week strikes the perfect balance—it's enough to keep the language fresh in your mind without leading to burnout. Plus, regular movement can boost overall brain health, making your learning sessions even more effective.

Bridging the Mind-Body Gap – Tips for Integrating Movement

- **Stay Engaged:** Use gestures, act out phrases, or even use props to make the learning process more dynamic.
- **Play Games:** Turn language exercises into physical games. For instance, a scavenger hunt where you name objects in your target language.
- **Story Time Actions:** When telling or listening to stories, incorporate relevant actions. This method helps cement vocabulary by linking it to physical activities.

Ease'On Down the Kinesthetic Path

Embarking on this journey might prompt others to wonder why you're watching children's shows with such enthusiasm or talking to yourself while jumping around. Yet, remember, by integrating movement with language learning, you're tapping into a powerful method that mirrors the natural learning experiences of children. This approach isn't just about imitating children; it's about reactivating a holistic way of learning that involves all senses, including your sense of motion.

Embracing the Inner Child

Embarking on this strategy might raise some eyebrows. "You're watching what? Hanging out with who?" But remember, every child was once a language learner, and they aced it. So, by channeling your inner child or just spending time with one, you're accessing that innate, intuitive method of learning. As for the cartoons? Think about it. Vivid visuals, repetitive themes, catchy tunes - it's almost as if they were tailor-made for language acquisition, right! So, to all the brave souls ready to jump into the wacky world of kids and cartoons

– I salute you! Dive in with gusto, enjoy the simplicity, the laughter, and the unabashed joy of childhood. Because when it comes to languages, sometimes, the youngest teachers are the wisest.

Remember: This is all REAL NEUROSCIENCE, backed up and peer-reviewed by doctors & scientists. With YOU already FLUENT in your native language & every kid out there learning your mother tongue as living proof of concept! I also know these works because I have used them personally to become fluent over & over again in multiple languages. So keep active, stay playful, and soon, you'll find yourself fluent in more ways than one. I can see 'future you' chatting away in your new language like it's child's play. After all, if a toddler can seamlessly combine learning with playtime, why not you?

BREW & STEW WITH NATIVE SPEAKERS

Culinary & Caffeinated Conversations

Imagine strolling through the aromatic lanes of a local market with your Coach, conversing about ingredients in your target language. You're not just learning now; you're living the language. The experiences – bargaining for fresh produce, discussing recipes – now become linguistic anchors.

Delve Deeper: Chronicle a simple market visit: narrate dialogues with your coach, cultural faux pas, and culinary discoveries, all provide you with a taste of real-world interactions. Delineate the potency of situational learning, perhaps experiencing in real life Stephen Krashen's Input Hypothesis, demonstrating how comprehensible input in authentic contexts (like bargaining) accelerates linguistic prowess.

Caffeine and Cuisine: Your Passport to Fluency

Alright, adventurers of the linguistic world! Prepare to discuss more deeply a chapter that's as delightful to your taste buds as it is to your language neurons. If you've got a soft spot for a good cup of green tea or enjoy chopping, stirring, and sizzling in the kitchen (or even if you burn toast and can't differentiate between a cappuccino and a latte), this part of the chapter is gonna be a flavorful ride. 🔍☕

Welcome to "Coffee with Coach"! ☕

What's that? You've been hunkering down with textbooks and apps? My friend, nothing screams a 'casual conversation starter' like coffee. Why? Well, because coffee shops are the modern-day epicenters of culture, where people trade and exchange ideas, and occasionally, passive-aggressive fights for power outlets to charge their devices. Lol

Here's the scoop (or should I say the brew?):

- **Natural Conversations:** No rehearsed lines. No set topics. Just good ol' spontaneous chats. Maybe about the weather, the latest football match, or why the barista can never get your name right.
- **Cultural Dive:** Ever noticed how coffee culture varies? Italians with their espressos, Swedes with fika, Turks with their strong brews. Every sip tells a tale.
- **Everyday Vocabulary:** Ordering coffee, talking about preferences, or even discussing the ambiance of the café - these conversations arm you with vocabulary you'll use regularly.
- **Real-time Feedback:** With every confused look, every

"Come again?" or every chuckle at your attempt to make a coffee pun, you get instant feedback.

Feeling Peckish? Let's "Cook with Coach"!

Whipping up a storm in the kitchen isn't just a sensory delight; it's a linguistic fiesta! Think about it. Fresh ingredients, colorful produce, the sound of sizzling, and the rich aroma – it's a multi-sensory experience, a fabulous backdrop for language practice.

Here's the recipe for success:

- **Market Madness:** Ah, the local market! A cacophony of voices, a palette of colors, and a crash course in negotiation in your target language. From asking for prices to understanding quantities, you'll be rolling in real-world vocabulary, together with your coach.
- **Step-by-step Cooking:** As you navigate through a recipe, you'll come across action verbs, kitchen vocabulary, and the wonderful world of taste descriptors. Salty, savory, spicy, or sinfully sweet - let your tongue learn in more ways than one.
- **Cultural Cuisine:** Every dish has a story, a history. As you cook, you'll not only learn about ingredients and techniques but also dive into tales, traditions, and perhaps even some tantalizing tidbits about grandma's secret recipe.
- **Bond Over Food:** Sharing a meal is universal. As you break bread (or tortillas, naan, rice – you get the picture), you'll find conversations flowing effortlessly.

Maximizing "Coffee & Cooking with Coach" Sessions

- *Play it safe, not sorry:* Always choose a verified and experienced language coach from a reputable company. Safety first, coffee (or delicious tea) second!
- *Embrace Mistakes:* Ordered a cold brew when you wanted an extra hot one? Accidentally used salt instead of sugar? Laugh it off. These bloopers will be the stories you'll fondly recount later.
- *Ask Questions:* Whether at the café or in the kitchen, be inquisitive. What's this dish called? Where do I purchase these specific ingredients? How do you say "delicious" in your language?
- *Take Notes:* Got a smartphone? Of course, you do. Whip it out, note down new words, interesting phrases, or maybe that recipe you just learned.
- *Engage All Your Senses:* Feel the coffee beans, smell the herbs, listen to the sound of frothing milk, watch the color of the stew change to a different hue, and taste, well, everything!

Bringing It All Together – The Java-Jive & Culinary Crossover

Now, you might be thinking, "This sounds lovely, but what if I'm a tea person?" or "I once burned instant noodles; can I really cook?" Here's the secret: it's not about the coffee or the cooking; it's about immersion in genuine, authentic experiences.

Imagine this: You walk into a café, greeted by the rich aroma of freshly ground coffee. You order your favorite beverage in your target language, maybe you mess it up a bit, but the barista smiles and corrects you. While waiting, you strike up a conversation with the person next to you in line waiting for their drink. You laugh, you learn, and you leave the café a tad more fluent than before.

Cut to the market. The hustle-bustle energizes you. You ask for fresh basil, learn it's called something entirely different in the local language, haggle a bit, and share a light moment with the vendor. Then, in the kitchen, as you and your coach navigate through a recipe, you're not just cooking; you're crafting memories. You're not just tasting flavors; you're tasting cultures.

A Toast to Tangible Learning!

If the previous strategies were about flexing your cognitive muscles, this is about letting your hair down, dancing in the kitchen, making a few coffee spills, and enjoying the symphony of flavors and phonetics. "Coffee with Coach" and "Cooking with Coach" aren't just lessons; they're experiences. They're the delightful interludes in your language-learning opera. So, whether you're a caffeine junkie or someone whose culinary skills are, let's say, a work in progress, this journey promises growth, giggles, and some gastronomic joy.

So, here's a challenge: By our next chapter, have a coffee story to share or a kitchen anecdote. A tiny tale of how you took the linguistic bull by the horns, with a cup of coffee (or tea) in one hand and a spatula in the other. Ready to Brew & Stew some fun?

LEND A HAND, LEARN A TON & THE HIDDEN GENIUS OF "SHOW & TELL" FOR ADULTS

Here's a brain-friendly tip that will flip your language learning process on its head: teaching others what you've learned isn't just good karma—it's one of the most effective ways to lock in all that new foreign language knowledge you've been soaking up.

You might be thinking, "Wait a second, I'm barely fluent myself, how can I teach anyone anything?" Well, stick with me here, because teaching others—whether it's explaining a word, walking someone through a tricky grammar rule, or just casually chatting about what you've learned—supercharges your learning in ways you wouldn't believe.

Delve Deeper: Take some extra time to reflect on your life's experiences and what you have learned so far about your target language & culture. After a teaching moment, take some time to reflect on what you learned and how it affected your language skills. This self-reflection will help reinforce your understanding and identify areas for improvement.

Make sure to practice with friends or family. Teach your friends or family members new words or phrases in your target language. Explain the meanings and contexts, and encourage them to use what they've learned from you.

Let's dig into the why, the how, and, of course, the science that backs this up. This is where things get exciting. We're not talking about some hypothetical benefit here; we're talking about *proven brain-boosting magic* that kicks into gear when you lend a hand to others.

The Power of the "Protege Effect"

Now, before you break into a cold sweat thinking of yourself as a language teacher, let me introduce you to something called the "protege effect." It's a fancy way of saying that when you teach something to someone else, you understand it better yourself. The effect is so powerful that it's been studied across many areas of learning—and language acquisition is no exception.

Researchers Fiorella and Mayer (2013) conducted a meta-analysis on this exact phenomenon. They found that when you teach others, your brain moves into a higher gear, organizing and processing information more effectively than it does when you're just studying alone. So, every time you explain something, even if it's just to a friend or fellow learner, you're reinforcing your own understanding.

Here's how it works: When you teach someone, you're not just recalling information. You're actively retrieving it, rephrasing it, and presenting it in a way that makes sense to another person. That process activates deeper cognitive functions in your brain, forcing you to think about what you know in a more structured way. It's like running your knowledge through a quality control check before passing it on.

And guess what? Every time you do this, you're building a stronger connection to the material in your own brain.

Show & Tell for Adults: Reinvented

Remember "Show & Tell" from elementary school? You brought in your favorite toy, showed it to the class, and then explained why it was awesome. As it turns out, that process wasn't just a way to get kids talking—it was a sneaky way to build language skills and confidence. So, why should we leave all that fun behind in childhood?

"Show & Tell" for adults is real, and here's why it works: teaching others makes us the main player in our learning journey. Imagine explaining a tricky verb tense to a friend who's also learning the language. You don't have to be an expert; just giving it a shot forces you to think more clearly about how the language works.

Even better? It activates your brain's retrieval and explanation mechanisms, both of which are key to long-term retention. In other words, every time you "show and tell" someone else what you've learned, you're not just helping them—you're rewiring your own brain for fluency.

And let's be honest: when you explain something to someone, you realize quickly where you might still be a little shaky. That's valuable feedback for YOU. It's not about being perfect; it's about improving as you go.

The Neuroscience Behind Teaching

Let's geek out on some brain science for a moment. Teaching taps into parts of the brain that studying alone just doesn't touch. A study by Hinds et al. (2011) showed that when you teach someone, it engages brain regions responsible for cognitive control and memory—places like the prefrontal cortex that help you organize and prioritize information.

In fact, when we teach, we activate neural pathways associated with executive functioning, making us better problem solvers. The act of teaching also improves your metacognition, which is just a fancy word for "thinking about your thinking." As you teach others, you start reflecting more on what you understand and what you don't—leading to better learning strategies.

You know how when you try to explain something complicated, you often end up understanding it better yourself? That's because your brain is working extra hard to organize that information for you *and* your "student." It's like you're giving your brain a workout every time you teach.

Teaching Others Means You're Practicing, Too

Remember, teaching doesn't mean giving a formal lesson. It's more about sharing what you know, no matter how small. Here's how it plays out in your language journey:

1. **Practice in Conversation**: Teaching someone can be as simple as sharing a new word you've learned with a friend or language partner. The act of explaining that word, how to use it, and putting it into context for them helps reinforce your understanding. You're engaging in active retrieval every time you do this, which strengthens your memory (Roediger & Butler, 2011).
2. **Explain Grammar Concepts**: Let's say you just figured out how to properly use a tricky verb tense. Go ahead and explain it to someone else! By teaching that concept to another person, you're not just helping them, you're also processing the information more deeply, which makes it stick in your brain longer (Fiorella & Mayer, 2013).
3. **Cultural Sharing**: Language and culture are deeply connected. So, as you pick up cultural insights, share those with others. When you explain why a particular gesture or phrase is used in a certain way, you're solidifying both the cultural and linguistic understanding. This kind of social interaction is key to language retention (Kumpulainen & Mutanen, 2005).

Collaborative Learning: Building a Fluency Community

Here's where it gets really fun—teaching language concepts doesn't have to be a one-way street. One of the best ways to make progress is to create a small community of fellow learners where you can share what you know and learn from each other. Think of it as a peer-to-peer learning setup. You explain something you've recently learned, and someone else shares their new insights with you.

This kind of collaborative learning, which Vygotsky (1978) would call the "Zone of Proximal Development," helps everyone push their limits. You're not just learning from textbooks—you're learning through interaction, which is a much more natural way to acquire a language.

Why This Habit Works: Lend A Hand, Learn A Ton

By now, you're probably starting to see why this habit is such a game-changer. It's not just about the act of teaching, but about what happens to your brain when you do it.

- **You deepen your understanding**: When you explain something to someone, your brain processes the information more deeply.
- **You reinforce memory**: Actively recalling and presenting information strengthens your memory pathways.
- **You build confidence**: Explaining new language concepts helps boost your confidence as a speaker.
- **You engage socially**: Teaching and sharing knowledge increases social interaction, which is crucial for language learning.
- **You become a better learner**: Through teaching, you enhance your metacognitive awareness—knowing what you know and what you still need to work on (Winne & Hadwin, 1998).

By teaching others, you're not only reinforcing your own learning, but you're also becoming part of a community that helps everyone thrive. It's about making the journey to fluency a shared experience, one where every conversation is a chance to learn—and teach.

References

- Fiorella, L., & Mayer, R. E. (2013). The effects of teaching on learning: A meta-analysis. *Educational Psychology Review*, 25(2), 181-206.
- Roediger, H. L., & Butler, A. C. (2011). The critical role of retrieval practice in long-term retention. *Trends in Cognitive Sciences*, 15(1), 20-27.
- Kumpulainen, K., & Mutanen, M. (2005). Interaction and learning in a peer-learning context. *Journal of Educational Psychology*, 97(3), 490-498.
- Hinds, O. C., et al. (2011). Neural correlates of knowledge exchange during the act of teaching. *Journal of Neuroscience*, 31(4), 1312-1319.
- Vygotsky, L. S. (1978). *Mind in Society: The Development of Higher Psychological Processes*. Harvard University Press.
- Winne, P. H., & Hadwin, A. F. (1998). Studying as self-regulated learning. *Self-Regulated Learning: Theory, Research, and Practice*, 27-28.

Volunteering: A Heartful & Linguistic Exchange

Within the warm embrace of sharing and contributing, language permeates through the heart's understanding. Volunteering, say at a local food bank where your target language is spoken, transforms every "thank you" and shared smile into meaningful, emotional linguistics.

Delve Deeper: Examine heartfelt stories of connection through linguistic mishaps and triumphs within volunteering. You can explore for yourself the psychology of emotional connections in learning, we'll also be providing research-backed commentary on how emotionally-charged experiences, like those in volunteering, enhance memory retention and linguistic application.

Volunteering: The Heart and Soul of Language Learning

Ahoj, linguistic thrill-seekers! Grab your superhero capes and philanthropic spirits, because we're diving deep into one of the most underrated yet fulfilling avenues for language learning in this part of the chapter: volunteering. This ain't just about adding a snazzy line to your resume or feeling a tad better about binge-watching that entire TV series last weekend. It's about immersing yourself in authentic conversations, building connections, and – surprise, surprise – getting heaps more on your language investment.

Why Volunteer? (Hint: It Ain't Just Altruism)

I hear you. "Isn't volunteering about giving?" Well, mi amigo, here's a secret. Volunteering is a sneaky little thing. Just when you think you're the Giver Supreme, dishing out love, time, and effort, you find yourself on the receiving end of a treasure trove of benefits, especially in the linguistic arena.

- *Authentic Conversations:* No scripted dialogues, no robotic responses. When you're distributing meals, painting walls, or organizing books, you're also trading stories, laughs, and sometimes, even the odd recipe or two.
- *Cultural Insights:* As you rub shoulders with the locals, you not only learn their language but also their customs, values, and traditions. Ever wondered why a particular festival is celebrated or the story behind that song? Just ask!

- *Vocabulary Expansion:* You'll pick up a ton of new words and phrases, especially those not found in textbooks. Expect a hearty mix of colloquialisms, slang, and just everyday chat.
- *Warm Fuzzies:* Beyond language, volunteering offers a massive boost to your mood, self-worth, and overall outlook on life. Dopamine, anyone?

Choosing Your Volunteering Gig

Now, before you dash off in a blaze of goodwill, it's essential to pick the right volunteering opportunity. After all, you want something that aligns with your interests, gives you ample opportunity to chat, and doesn't involve deciphering ancient alien languages (unless that's your thing).

- *Teaching:* If you've got the patience and passion, teaching is fabulous. Whether it's English, math, music, or mimes, you're in for some fantastic student-teacher banter.
- *Food Banks or Soup Kitchens:* Apart from the obvious feel-goods, these places are buzzing hives of activity and chatter. Perfect for the sociable linguist!
- *Community Events:* Be it a carnival, a concert, or a conference on the virtues of vegetarian vampires, events are a goldmine for random, delightful conversations.
- *Elderly Care Homes:* Oldies have stories, wisdom, and a gift for gab. Plus, they're generally patient and love a keen listener. Win-win!

Navigating the Volunteering Voyage

Now that you've donned your volunteering hat (and perhaps a pair of snazzy gloves). Here's how to maximize this journey:

- *Be Genuine:* No one likes anyone that's fake. Come with an open heart and the intent to contribute. The language benefits? They'll flow naturally.
- *Ask Away:* Channel that inner curious child. Why is this done this way? How do you pronounce that? What's the history here?
- *Join Groups:* Many volunteer organizations have teams. A diverse group promises a wider range of conversations and insights.
- *Share Your Stories:* As much as you're there to soak in the vibe, don't shy away from sharing. It's a two-way street, after all.

Tales from the Trenches

Picture this: You're at a community garden, trying to figure out the difference between a carrot and a parsnip (they're trickier than they look). You turn to a fellow volunteer – a native speaker – and embark on a hilarious, hands-on tutorial on root vegetables, complete with anecdotes of carrot-induced accidents and parsnip pies.

Cut to another day: You're at a local event, attempting to set up a stall, but for the life of you, can't figure out how to pronounce the items you're selling. A little kid, barely waist high, comes up and corrects your accent, leaving you both in with the LOL 😂 emoji all over your face.

Such tales aren't just anecdotes; they're milestones in your linguistic journey. The day you managed to haggle in the local lingo, the time you made a room erupt in laughter with a well-timed joke, or when you consoled someone in their native tongue – these are the markers of your growth, not just as a learner, but as a global citizen.

A Bow of Gratitude

Volunteering is like that hearty, homemade stew – it warms you from the inside, fills you up in more ways than one, and leaves a lingering taste of something beautiful. It's not just about language; it's about the stories you weave, the bonds you form, and the sheer, unadulterated joy of giving and receiving in equal measure.

As we close on this section, here's your challenge: Step out, find a cause close to your heart, and dive into the delightful chaos of volunteering. Trust me, in this linguistic exchange program, you'll always get more than you give. And, as you navigate this maze of words, emotions, and connections, always remember to wear your most genuine smile and carry a pocketful of gratitude.

Ready to volunteer your way to fluency? Off you go, Captain Kindheart!

UNLEASHING YOUR LANGUAGE SUPERPOWERS: A SYMPHONY OF INFLUENCES

Jim Kwik: The Brain Maestro

In the grand symphony of language acquisition, Jim Kwik takes center stage as the virtuoso of memory mastery. His insights into brain optimization and memory enhancement create a crescendo that echoes through the corridors of language learning. As we navigate the linguistic labyrinth, Kwik's teachings become our guiding notes, harmonizing effortlessly with the principles of FluentBrain.Me.

> *"Knowledge is not power. Knowledge is potential power. Action is power."*

> *"Limitations live only in our minds. But if we use our imaginations, our possibilities become limitless."*

Kwik's mantra becomes our anthem, reminding us that intelligence isn't a fixed entity but a dynamic landscape waiting to be explored. As we adopt the "✋FluentBrain Habits," we dance to the rhythm of unlocking our cognitive potential, seamlessly integrating Kwik's neuroscientific wisdom into our language journey.

Dr. Paul Pimsleur: The Melodious Mentor

Enter the realm of language cadence with Dr. Paul Pimsleur, the maestro behind the Pimsleur Method. His legacy echoes in every FluentBrain.Me lesson, transforming language learning into a melodic journey. Pimsleur's approach aligns with the heart of our methodology – repetition, immersion, and the art of listening.

> *"Words are the building blocks of communication, but understanding the culture behind them is what truly brings them to life."*

> *"Language learning should be a natural process; it should feel like playing, not studying."*

In tandem with the "✋FluentBrain Habits," Pimsleur's philosophy becomes our compass. We don't just learn words; we embrace language as a living, breathing, ever-evolving conduit. As we bounce to the linguistic symphony, Pimsleur's teachings seamlessly intertwine with our pursuit of fluency, creating a harmonious duet that resonates in every conversation.

Johnny Harris: The Visual Voyager

We are now well on our way, traversing through the vast landscapes of language, Johnny Harris becomes our visual compass, guiding us through the cultural tapestry that words alone cannot capture. FluentBrain.Me, embraces the genius behind Harris's immersive storytelling, transforming language learning into a visual feast. Harris's knack for uncovering stories within stories aligns with our ethos as well – language as a cultural narrative.

> *"The best stories happen at the intersection of curiosity and creativity."*
>
> *"When you put yourself out there, you invite the world to share in your journey."*

With the " FluentBrain Habits" in tow, we delve into narratives, not just textbooks. We absorb the nuances of language through the lens of culture, creating a visual vocabulary that extends beyond words. Harris's influence becomes our lens, enhancing our ability to see, feel, and truly understand the soul of our language.

Dr. Daniel Amen: The Mindful Maestro

Embarking on the linguistic expedition, we carry the teachings of Dr. Daniel Amen as our mindfulness guide. Amen's insights into brain health and holistic well-being intertwine seamlessly with the philosophy here within our boutique service. As we adopt the " FluentBrain Habits," we become not just bilingual, trilingual & multilingual people, but mindful navigators, attuned to the connection between mental well-being and linguistic prowess.

"The key to a better life is to take better care of your brain."

"Your brain is not the thing that you have, it is the thing that you are."

Amen's words echo in our journey, prompting us to approach language learning not just as a mental exercise but as a holistic transformation. Our platform becomes not just a language institute but a sanctuary for mental flourishing, where language learning is a journey of self-discovery.

Rachel Paling: The Cultural Connector

In the grand tapestry of Brain-Friendly Language Learning, Rachel Paling stands as the architect of cultural connectivity. Her expertise in Neurolanguage Coaching® becomes the cornerstone of our approach here. Paling's emphasis on coaching aligns seamlessly with our commitment to personalized guidance just for you. As we sip coffee with our coach or explore markets with native speakers, Paling's influence becomes our compass for bridging language and culture together.

"The brain works better in a curiosity state, and increases activity in the hippocampus, which I call "The Memory Master".

Curiosity in essence is the drive which humans possess to discover, unravel, explore, and learn."

"I believe that a deeper comprehension will lead to humanity communicating together in a totally different way, developing new ways of living and moving forward"

Paling's philosophy also becomes our North Star, guiding us beyond language proficiency into the realm of cultural mastery. FluentBrain.Me is NOT a language course **in itself** but rather a neuroscientific voyage where every word learned is a step toward creating a future rich in intercultural understanding.

Connecting the Dots: Leading Your Own Symphony

As the curtain rises on your linguistic saga, we realize that these maestros – Kwik, Pimsleur, Harris, Amen, and Paling – are not mere influences but integral leaders in the grand symphony of your language acquisition. And here, our Digital Courses become the stage where their teachings converge, creating a harmonious composition that resonates in every lesson, coaching session, and cultural immersion.

"It can be said that we often know more about HOW our smartphone works or more about HOW the automobile we drive works than HOW the single MOST IMPORTANT device in our entire life works, OUR BRAIN... Your potential can be LIMITLESS. Just imagine what your life would look like, if you discovered you have a new "Super Power" tomorrow...!

Our passion here at FluentBrain is to help each one of you understand HOW YOUR OWN BRAIN FUNCTIONS during the language learning process, so that you now MASTER your own path to SUCCESS...

Very much like when you first learned to ride a bicycle, once you've learned to ride one bike, it's safe to say you have essentially learned HOW to ride ALL bikes. (Remember it's the process, not the bike...Lol) It doesn't matter if it's a BMX or a Harley-Davidson... Same goes for learning HOW to drive a car. It doesn't matter if it's a Ford Fiesta or a Ferrari Testarossa.

Your brain has now MASTERED THE PROCESS."
"Learning a new language is not just about new vocabulary or
*grammar rules; it's about using your hands to weave **YOUR***
***OWN** story, it's about understanding the SOUL of the language,*
the culture, and connecting to the HEART of the people."

- Ryan Johnson / Founder of FluentBrain.Me

With the "5 FluentBrain Habits" as our sheet music and FluentBrain.Me as your orchestra, we embark on a journey together where every word learned, every cultural insight gained, and every connection made contributes to the grand opus of your multilingual potential.

Our method is the BRIDGE between WHERE YOU ARE NOW AND WHERE YOU WANT TO BE. Combining the best of linguistic neuroscience, psychological insights, and practical applications, custom-designed just for you. It's your roadmap to becoming not just proficient but FLUENT and CONFIDENT in your new language. So, allow YOUR symphony to continue, click over to our website and may the language maestros guide you to new heights of fluency and cultural mastery. 🎶🌐

WHY CONTINUE YOUR JOURNEY WITH US HERE AT FLUENTBRAIN.ME...?

Embark on the Next Leg of Your Language Adventure with FluentBrain.Me! 🚀

Introduction: Unleash Your Multilingual Potential

Hey Language Legend! If you've reached this page of our book, you're not merely on a linguistic stroll; you're on a thrilling adventure to master the art of communication. With our unique position & experience, we don't just coach you through your languages, we empower you to become the master of your own destiny; think of us as the base programming that runs as an ESSENTIAL FUNCTION of your computer, think of us as the updated operating system on your new smartphone that allows you to communicate with the world around you. It's only after your device has its base operating system, that you can now load all your favorite apps on your phone, even language apps, including the FLUENZ App on the App Store; we cultivate a mindset, a lifestyle, pass-porting you to new realms of understanding. So, why continue your journey with us? Let's unravel the tapestry of FluentBrain.Me and the vibrant world of possibilities awaiting you.

A Symphony of Learning Styles: Because One Size Doesn't Fit All

Remember that "aha!" moment when you finally grasped a tricky concept? At FluentBrain.Me, we celebrate those moments! We understand that every language explorer is unique. Whether you're a visual virtuoso, an auditory aficionado, or a hands-on hero, our courses are crafted to harmonize with YOUR learning style. It's not just about learning; it's about savoring the journey, and we've got the perfect melody for you.

Native Speaker Nirvana: Immerse Yourself in Authenticity

Imagine learning French from a Parisian in a bustling café or picking up Japanese from a Tokyo native under the neon lights of the city. FluentBrain.Me brings you closer to the heart of a language through immersive experiences with native speakers. No stilted dialogues; just real conversations that resonate from the heart with the authenticity of everyday life. Get ready to absorb language like a local and discover the cultural nuances that text-books miss.

The FluentBrain Community: Where Language Lovers Unite

Learning a language is not a solitary pursuit; it's a communal celebration! At FluentBrain.Me, you're not just a student; you're part of a global community fueled by passion and curiosity. Join forums, attend virtual & live in-person meetups, and engage with fellow language enthusiasts. Swap stories, share victories, and find inspiration in the mosaic of experiences that make up our vibrant community.

Coaching that Clicks With You: Personalized Guidance for Your Language Odyssey

Ever wished for a personal language sherpa? Look no further! FluentBrain.Me offers personalized coaching sessions tailored to your journey. Coffee with Coach & Cooking with Coach – think of it as not just language lessons but cultural adventures with your personal guide. Break free from the constraints of conventional learning, and let our coaches be your companions on this exhilarating expedition.

Multifaceted Fluency: Go Beyond Words to Enter Cultural Mastery

Fluency isn't just about words; it's about embodying the essence of a language. Our courses at FluentBrain.Me go beyond vocabulary drills and grammar rules. We guide you through the cultural labyrinth, ensuring you not only speak the language but also understand the unspoken. It's the difference between just ordering coffee and savoring it at a corner boulangerie in Paris – an experience that's sure to transcend words.

Cutting-Edge Learning Techniques: Tomorrow's Tools for Today's Learners

Step into the future of language learning! FluentBrain.Me leverages cutting-edge technology to make your learning experience seamless and enjoyable. From interactive lessons in applied neuroscience scenarios to gamified challenges, we've curated an arsenal of tools that align with the neuroplasticity of the modern learner. Say goodbye to monotony and hello to dynamic, brain-friendly language mastery.

Mindful Learning: Where Progress Meets Pleasure

Learning a language should be enjoyable, not arduous. Our courses at FluentBrain.Me infuse an element of play into the process. Explore language through songs, engage with stories, and let your linguistic curiosity lead the way. We believe that joyful learning is sustainable learning, and your journey with us is designed to be as delightful as it is enlightening. - Just like it was the first time you learned a language!

Your Passport to Infinite Horizons

So, why continue your journey with FluentBrain.Me? Because here, you're not just a language learner; you're a conversation starter, a multilingual team leader, and that cool family member who finally understands all your in-law's jokes.

Remember, whether you're eyeing that dream job abroad, simply craving to connect with your multilingual family, or gearing up for more globetrotting, FluentBrain.Me is your gateway to infinite horizons.

Are you ready to turn the page to the next chapter of your language adventure? Join us and leverage our expertise, where fluency meets brain-friendly fun, and the world becomes your playground. Your multilingual saga awaits – let's put pen to paper - together!

CONCLUSION

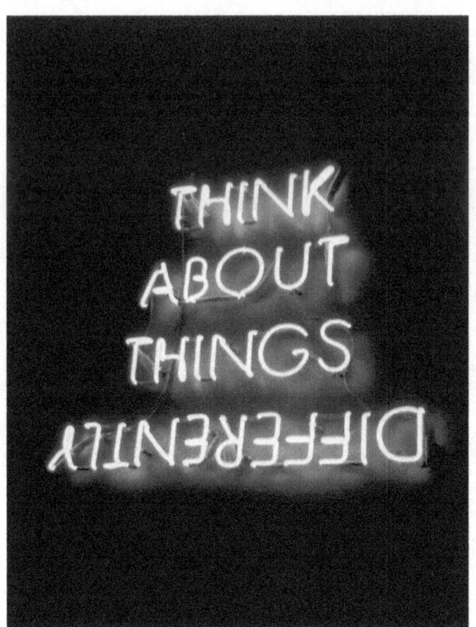

We have this idea that children can learn better than adults. We think they have no problem with adding another language to their resume. But what's really the point to be made about children and adults learning a new language?

When learning a new language, both adults and children have their own unique strengths andlimitations.

- A controlled learning environment benefits adults more than it benefits children.

Adults and teenagers acquire almost every language skill quicker than youngsters, according to research. Isn't it interesting, to say the least? In comparison to youngsters, they have a better command of grammar, vocabulary, reading comprehension, and the ability to articulate more complicated thoughts. Adults have lived and learned; they know how to study and now (after reading this book) they even know how their memory works. They may have a better understanding of the meaning of words and have uncovered numerous parallels by using their home language. When it comes to learning a new language, adults have several advantages over youngsters.

A common misconception is that learning a new language is most difficult beyond a certain age. This one concept is harming adult language learners throughout the world.

Adults are masters of language acquisition. A simple response to the question, "Is it possible that I'm too old?" is no. Why, therefore, do so many people feel that children learn more quickly than adults? Let's take a look at it.

- Children's pronunciation skills are superior.

Children have an advantage when it comes to accurately reproducing regional accents. When youngsters are younger, they are more likely to be able to imitate foreign noises. Adults have a harder time replicating new sounds than children do. As a result, it seems that they are more proficient in the new language they are learning. This ability tends to diminish with age, and as a result, we have a much more difficult time recreating sounds that are utterly foreign to us. Children have this as their most significant advantage compared to adults. The good news is that IT HAS NO EFFECT ON FLUENCY AT ALL. Even if they have a detectable accent, adults CAN learn to speak a language fluently!

- Expectations of children and those of adults are in stark contrast.

The natural language vocabulary of an adult and a three-year-old toddler is vastly different. If the youngster learns only a few hundred words in the new language, he's already proficient since his original language has already caught up with him. To communicate complicated thoughts as fluently as in your mother tongue as an adult, you'll still need to master five times the vocabulary a youngster did. As adults, we don't recognize how good we are in our native tongue. To get to this point it has taken us a long time to get here. Therefore, learning a second or third language will also take some time to come up to speed.

- Self-Awareness as an Adult.

Adults, on the other hand, become self-conscious because of these high expectations. They don't want to seem foolish while communicating in a foreign language. Adults tend to avoid speaking a foreign language as much as possible. Young people couldn't appear to care less.

Even if infants have a minimal vocabulary, they begin to use the language immediately to express themselves. When they want some sweets, they just say "candy." As time passes, individuals become more conversant with the concept. Until we can say, "I'd like to taste your apple-cinnamon lollipop in the green box please. It's on the third shelf behind you," we're going to feel awkward. This is an area where we need to be more like children and accept our imperfections.

- As soon as a child sees something they like, they dive right in.

For youngsters, learning a second language is less common as a genuine interest or hobby. In many cases, children are forced to learn a new language because their parents have relocated or because they have been enrolled in an immersion program. Also, if a child wants to be accepted by their peers, they are often required to master new skills. Adults, however, usually put down roots like a tree and generally like to stay in their familiar surroundings. Even though they reside in a foreign city, adults somehow find a way to make acquaintances who speak their home language. At home, they converse in their mother tongue, watch TV, and read in their mother tongue. Immersion can be difficult for grown-ups. When it comes to learning a language, young children don't give it much thought; instead, they just jump right in with what they already know and pay attention to the people around them. They don't question whether or not they're improving or whether what they say is correct. THEY JUST DEVELOP AT THEIR OWN PACE.

While children have an advantage over adults, it is possible for adults to become more childlike in their learning techniques.

- Adults and Children both learn in a new way.

Adults are excellent at intentionally acquiring languages. A language-learning application like Fluenz Online Immersion may help them make tremendous progress WITHOUT a classroom. Unfortunately, this enormous power may also be a vulnerability. Due to the fact that they are so adept at absorbing information during lectures, they often stop there. They don't go to the movies, don't listen to music, don't meet new people, don't read great literature, and don't really use their new language. When it comes to learning your target language, exposure is critical. You'll be unstoppable if you can use your adult abilities to study intentionally from the many resources at your disposal while simultaneously utilizing the ability we all have from our youth to absorb languages instinctively.

- Remember to (Actively) Listen!

Learning a new language may be accomplished by either active or passive listening. Active listening is much more successful than passive listening in picking up new words and phrases. This is because active listening demands focus, attention, and speech. Yes, active listening requires actual words to come out of your mouth. I must say, that was a "light bulb moment" for me & the key to success for those of you learning a new language! On the other hand, you can learn as a passive listener as well, but passive listening is more passive. Now when you stop and think about it… How many children do you know that are passive listeners? Kids are great active listeners! And they do a great job mimicking & imitating others, which is not only fun, but it's a secret to becoming a fluent speaker fast.

Benny Lewis, an Irish Polyglot and a language specialist says that language has to be taken care of (Polizzi, 2018). Your full attention is paid to the phrases that are being uttered while you are speaking with a buddy in your relaxed home colloquialisms, for example. When you start multitasking, your focus moves to a new task, and it becomes more difficult to remember what occurred before you started doing so. If you want to keep up with native speakers, you'll need to practice paying attention to what they're saying and giving it your complete attention.

The Japanese language specialist John Fotheringham advises beginning students to spend time actually SPEAKING their language rather than merely studying it (Polizzi, 2018). As a result, while practicing active listening, it's crucial to focus on what native speakers are saying & their meaning. As a beginner in a new language, you may find it hard to keep up with the conversational tempo of native speakers. Fortunately, according to Fotheringham, the best and probably quickest method to learn a language is to listen to real information.

There is nothing better than listening to a podcast from a native speaker to boost your listening comprehension. Lindsay Do Languages recommends listening to French music and listening to French podcasts to increase listening comprehension. Even if you're sitting at your work or traveling in your vehicle, listening to music, podcasts, and radio programs may help you improve your active listening abilities.

I can really say that this has been true in my case. There was one instance while driving in my car during work to my service area. While in the car, driving in between each client I would visit, I had the radio tuned into a station speaking in my target language.

As the radio announcer transitioned into a topic about different foods, I heard the name of a food that I had never heard before. But I could definitely tell by the way they described this food, that it was so yummy and it was one of my favorite fruits. The two people kept referring to it as "Niu You Guo" which, when translated, means "butter fruit". So I started to think about what fruit this could be, and suddenly I thought, "Avocado"! Because its texture is smooth and creamy like butter, but in the shape of a fruit or small melon.

I have had many experiences like this that have increased my vocabulary and improved my fluency in my multiple target languages. All because I chose to actively listen & build a listening routine every day.

- Build a listening routine for your language

It's time to get into the habit of actively listening each day, just like kids growing up around you. In her Language Habit Toolkit, blogger, teacher, and podcaster Kerstin Cable offers a variety of practical suggestions for improving one's language skills (Polizzi, 2018). According to Cable, establishing a schedule is critical for anybody interested in learning a foreign language. A successful routine is built on a foundation of consistency and attention. According to her, "Building a language habit is the ideal method for progressive improvement, as well as enabling oneself to bring pleasure and sustainability to language study."

Cable recommends focusing on basic, attainable improvements and attainable objectives in order to develop a habit. Active listening activities are an excellent method to immerse yourself in local speech as part of your language study regimen. The most practical method to engage oneself in active listening is to practice little doses over days, weeks, and months.

NEVER GET INTIMIDATED AGAIN

The first step in mastering a new language is to set fluency aside (whatever that means for you). If your objective is one that will take years to attain, it's easy to get discouraged. Setting objectives that are attainable and quantifiable is essential to learning a new language. When learning a new language, don't go out on your first jog with the intention of running a marathon: instead, focus on short-term objectives that will give you a feeling of accomplishment. An excellent place to start is by learning the alphabet or a small number of characters and then moving on to learning a few basic phrases.

You may set new objectives as you make progress and begin to achieve them, such as being able to converse with a native speaker or reading a news item. A textbook doesn't have to dictate your objectives; you don't have to learn colors or vocations just now. Instead, focus on learning only the most essential vocabulary, like the verbs "so," "then," and "but," which are used often in everyday speech. In a short period, you will become so familiar with these strange little words & phrases as the sounds of these new words brushing against your ears will start to become more and more commonplace, and suddenly these words for "but" "then" & "so" won't really feel so foreign to you anymore, but rather will naturally flow from your mouth as you express yourself more fluently. Setting learning objectives can help you become more adept at analyzing your personal language requirements and pinpointing precisely what you need to study NEXT at each step of your journey throughout the language.

Identifying objectives necessitates figuring out a strategy for achieving them. A lot of attention is paid to selecting languages to study, but it's easy to overlook the process of learning a new language. While in school, your instructor would be responsible for deciding what you learn and when, so you may not have had to think about the method or technique as much. Then, as an independent student, you have had to plan out for yourself how you'll get there. So, ask yourself WHY you want to learn a new language in the first place. Are you expecting to meet locals while on vacation, or are you hoping to read a book that hasn't been translated?

Having a clear idea of what you want to accomplish can help you choose the best strategies to become fluent fast. Language for particular purposes has been around for a long time, allowing learners who require a new language for a job, or to communicate with family members, or even for their university studies. This is not a new discovery. However, in each language, its basic tenets may be used by non-native speakers as well. To begin, ask yourself what you want to be able to do with your new language.

In addition, strategies are critical. What works for me may not work for you; thus, there is no one-size-fits-all strategy for learning a new language! Even if you despise doing written tasks from a textbook, you don't have to let it stop you from succeeding in your fluency. I've noticed that public libraries typically have all-audio methods like those pioneered by Michel Thomas and Dr. Pimsleur (and supplied FOR FREE IN MULTIPLE LANGUAGES). When I began studying Chinese, I was introduced to Pimsleur's rhythmic tones. After walking 30 minutes to and from work every day one summer, I couldn't believe a course existed that just needed me to listen, think, and talk while leaving me with an intuitive comprehension of Chinese verbs.

LEARNING LIKE A KID AGAIN

Is it actually the case that children have an easier time learning new languages than adults?

It's possible that this is the case at the beginning. When it comes to learning a new language, many psychologists and educators believe that there is a key window of time called the "critical period," between the time of birth and the age of around 12 when it is easier for children to do so. In general, the higher the chances of comprehensive mastery of the language, the sooner the kid learns it.

Why is this the case?

Learning new words and grammar structures is easier in the early stages of life, when youngsters can detect and differentiate the sounds that make up their native language or languages, and their brains are ready to learn new ones. Overall, a child's ability to learn is greatly influenced by their developmental stage. The youngsters will be able to make sense of what they hear if they are exposed to a second, third, and even multiple languages simultaneously.

The brain, on the other hand, changes and "prunes" itself as we age. Rather than rapidly absorbing information, it now uses the knowledge we already have within a predetermined framework. As a result, adults learn in a fundamentally different manner from children in many respects.

However, us adults can still learn a lot from youngsters regarding their attitude. So why not adopt a more childlike outlook instead of being frustrated? Even if you think you're being ridiculous, these tips will actually help you. The following are my top ideas for making learning a new language enjoyable and simple, whether you're studying French, Chinese, Spanish, Japanese, Korean, German, or any other language. If you combine these time-tested techniques with regular language classes, you'll be speaking like a native in no time.

- Laugh and Play as if you were a kid again!

Laughter is a natural part of childhood! Brain studies have shown that laughing and having a good time may help you recall information more effectively. In fact, it's generally better if you don't take learning a foreign language too seriously. Learn some goofy French, Spanish, and Japanese words and silly jokes. Be entertained. Take a look at the positive side of things! Aside from bringing you a sense of levity, these catchphrases and tongue twisters will serve as helpful study aids for bettering your own oral pronunciation. They might become stuck in your mind, so just be aware! Remember those things you used to rhyme together as a kid or the things your schoolmates would rhyme about on the playground?

Learn Spanish as though you were an 8-year-old kid! If you're up for a challenge, try "Tres tristes tigres tragaban trigo en un trigal," a poem about tigers. Try making it a competition with another Spanish newbie to see who will win 🏆.

Just remember why this is fun.

It's not unusual for youngsters to discover a subject or activity that interests them while engaged in playtime, even if it's only pretending. Children play in a manner that adults do not, although we may fantasize and have our own hobbies.

Remember to tailor your learning specific to you, think about real-life scenarios while you're practicing your target language. It's a fun way to learn Korean as a child does: imagine you're ordering food at a night market in Seoul. Consider how you would approach people and the foodstuffs you would choose.

That actually reminds me of an experience I had in an Asian night market while living in Taipei, Taiwan. Navigating an Asian night market is definitely an experience to remember! And you weave in and out of the crowds, the aromas of freshly prepared dishes, steamy, crispy, sizzling spices waft across your nose, just above the voices of midnight foodies enjoying the treasures of their culinary quest in the darkness. The smells and tastes entice you in every direction, making it hard to decide which tasty path to choose.

One evening while on the prowl for spicy fried tofu, I encountered some new phrases that would allow me to 'up my game', and take my tasty food journey to a whole new level. The kind woman preparing my tasty treat looks at me and suddenly asks, "Ni Yao La Bu La," which, when loosely translated, means, "do you want it a little spicy or a lot spicy?"

I responded with a single word, "La." And boy, did I feel the results of not taking the seriousness of that word to heart! Haha… The result was my mouth burning so hot that you could see the flames shooting off my tongue!

So you bet the next time I visited the night market I definitely responded to my favorite spicy fried tofu lady with a polite "Bu La Xie Xie", and was very happy with my meal.

Remember to take lessons in your target language toward something you want to do, such as cooking, music, sailing, family, career, travel, etc. This can be done more easily if you find yourself in another country, but it's not necessary. You can also do things to make your foreign language feel LESS foreign right there in your very own city!

Transform your home into a language-learning lab. Immerse yourself in your new language without needing to travel. Practice techniques like labeling your surroundings, engaging with different types of media in your target language, and incorporating language practice into your daily routines, making your learning journey as natural as breathing the air around you.

Another option is to contact a Local or Online Coach who is fluent in your target language and teaches the activity you find enjoyable. This form of Adult "Play" may also stimulate your mind and increase your creativity, whether you are making up imaginary situations or taking part in real-life activities.

- Learn the language by immersing yourself in it.

Everywhere you turn, your native or target language is being spoken all around you. An immersion program or a journey to a location where the language you want to learn is spoken may help you achieve your goal. You may also improve your language skills by associating with others who are fluent in the language or are actively studying it. However, you don't need to go halfway across the world to take advantage of this advice. You may be amazed at how many chances there are to practice a language in your local area. Make friends in your neighborhood and start looking into your alternatives.

To learn Spanish like a kid, you may choose a restaurant where native speakers work and eat. Start a discussion over a meal and a drink! See if they have any suggestions for the cuisine or just try something that catches your eye. In most cases, native speakers are glad to assist those of you who want to improve your language skills.

- Incorporate stories and music into the framework of your instruction.

Do some research online to find children's songs and stories written in your target language or that are for bilingual speakers. Atomic Habits, which has been translated into dozens of different languages, is an example of this. You'll be able to fill in the blanks better if you're familiar with the writing. New terms will be simpler to learn if you're acquainted with the subject matter already.

Children, too, like re-reading and re-listening to good stories. With each repeat, we reinforce what we've learned, which helps us better grasp the tale and retain our new language. You'll be reading chapter novels in no time if you start with fairy tales or picture books.

Adults can learn, too, if they have the necessary resources. Some of the most outstanding individuals on this planet have a passion for learning and are always looking for new ways to improve themselves. The challenge of learning a new language later in life may be greater, but it's never impossible. The best way to start learning a language like a kid is to enroll in online language courses with a coach. Learn your target language with the help of a NeuroLanguage Coach and harness your inner child to achieve MASSIVE success.

PUT STREAMING SERVICES TO GOOD USE

You're already enjoying your Netflix, Hulu, AppleTV+, etc. Don't forget to use the things you're most comfortable with as a way to learn your new language.

When learning a new language, immersing yourself in the culture is the most effective method to do it. There are several reasons for this, including the fact that persons who acquire a new language while living outside of their own country become proficient more quickly. The logic is sound: if you use the language you're learning on a daily basis, you'll quickly improve your proficiency. For the majority of individuals, learning a new language abroad is out of the question. The internet, on the other hand, makes it quite simple to locate information in a language other than English. Plenty of content is available to stream, including Netflix originals and YouTube videos. Watching the show, Friends, for the 20th time is a great way to learn a new language!

- Watch Familiar Movies & TV Shows Dubbed in Your Target Language with Subtitles in your Native Language

Make sure to switch on the subtitles when you're viewing a program or video in your target language. When you read the subtitles together with the conversation, you'll begin to make connections between the words and expressions. You'll know how to say "thank you" in Portuguese if you hear the phrase "obrigado" every time a character says it. It's a terrific way to broaden your vocabulary, even if it doesn't assist with reading or writing.

- Voice-Overs

It's best to view stuff in its original language while you're trying to learn a new language. If you want to learn Japanese, for example, you should watch subtitled anime rather than English dubs. Watching it in Japanese with English subtitles is a great way to pick up new words and idioms. If you choose the dubbed version, on the other hand, you will miss out on important information.

This also applies to Netflix originals that you've marked for viewing. Watching, La Casa de Papel (Money Heist) in Spanish with English subtitles is a superior option. If you want to learn a new language quickly, this strategy is better than viewing English television with subtitles in a different language. Dark (German), Kingdom (Korean), Selection Day (Indian), Call My Agent! (French) and 3% are more international Netflix series worth checking out.

- Become acquainted with YouTubers from other countries.

Everywhere you look, there's a YouTube channel dedicated to a language you're studying. Listening to ordinary people talk about their lives on YouTube is a great way to learn about other cultures. Because of this, you'll acquire contemporary idioms and current terminology in addition to improving your pronunciation. YouTube even offers the ability to translate videos automatically. Due to bugs and occasional translation errors, it's not a great way to learn for individuals who don't spend much time on the platform.

FINAL THOUGHTS

In the beginning, learning a new language might be quite difficult for some. As a foreign language, you must acquire new vocabulary, as well as the structure of sentences and the verb tenses used in them, also the culture's distinctive phrases and idioms. It's extremely rewarding since we often learn new things when we try to overcome difficulties.

First and foremost, embrace the idea that you will progressively improve your proficiency in the language if you continue to expose yourself to it. Even if you don't realize it, you're becoming better & better with each day that passes. You and your new language will get to know each other better. Certain idioms, Nouns, a few connector words, and many forms of verbs become increasingly familiar to the brain with time. Even if you can't get every single one of them, you'll become used to them with time.

Avoid putting things off! Get yourself moving forward!

Don't give up on this. Recognize that speaking understandable language requires a lot of actual speaking. An In-Person Coach or meeting with a NeuroLanguage Coach online can keep you improving your language skills if you chat with them once or twice a week, or even more often.

You should be grateful & feel proud of all the wonderful progress that you are making. If you're increasing your vocabulary and understanding, you're increasing your potential. If you're forced to use the language often, you'll rapidly enhance your proficiency. Take advantage of the chance to speak out-loud when it arises. Don't be afraid to voice your mind, even if you make errors. It doesn't matter what anybody else thinks about it. As a fluent speaker, you must put yourself in that situation at some point, right?

Make use of the environment around you by thinking of: How well do you know a native speaker of the language you'd want to learn? Has social media helped you locate a new friend? Why don't you try looking for a Language Coach? Having more chances to interact with actual people can connect you to the culture and help you become a better communicator.

A lot of speaking is necessary if you want to improve your talent and potential. It doesn't matter if you make errors when you talk a lot. Afterward, you can go back to your listening and reading with some challenging information and then some easy content to build up some fundamental phrases you can utilize in your communication. We'll just employ a tiny fraction of the vocabulary that we know in order to communicate effectively. Our active vocabulary will be considerably less than our passive vocabulary, but that's a good thing since you'll comprehend and your active vocabulary will grow over time, gradually.

Make sure your goals are S.M.A.R.T.

Specific - Measurable - Achievable - Relevant - Time Bound

Give yourself real goals. Have goals you can follow sustainably. Small enough to give you a little push, but not too huge where they are unreasonable. As a result of this experience over time, you'll become a better person. Secondly, don't be afraid to switch up the kind of stuff you listen to. The difficulty level or even type of the challenge may be varied. Those who like grammar should read about it. However, if you're a fan of language tests & games, don't limit yourself to them. Make sure to change things up and then hunt for chances to speak.

Do not expect to be able to speak fluently if you are not giving yourself enough opportunities to do so. Work on honing your skills to take full advantage of any opportunities that come your way. Do not worry about any mistakes, blunders, or shortcomings that you may encounter. Take advantage of this wonderful opportunity you have!

May you be PATIENT with yourself... May you reach for KINDNESS along your journey... And may you wake up each day feeling CONFIDENT, learning your new foreign language naturally, FEARLESSLY FLUENT, JUST LIKE A KIDDO!

PASS THE MIC TO THE NEXT LANGUAGE ROCKSTAR

Alright, language champ! You've danced your way through this book of languages, mingled with kids and probably had too many coffees with your Coach (as if there's such a thing as too much coffee!). Now, how about passing the baton and paving the way for another padawan linguist?

Here's a nifty idea: let's help them find the golden ticket to language fluency, TOGETHER. How, you ask? Just swing by Amazon and drop your two cents about this book. Sharing your experiences, insights, and even your most memorable "aha!" moments can be the perfect signpost for another aspiring polyglot, pointing them right to this treasure trove of language wisdom.

By doing so, you're not just leaving a review; you're building a bridge for others to cross the sometimes choppy waters of language learning. Kindly remember that YOUR REVIEW is their lifeline!

A Gargantuan Thank You! For your commitment to language, and now, sharing the love, keeps this linguistic journey pulsating with life. Every word of encouragement, every piece of feedback fuels our mission - making the world a smaller, more connected place, one language at a time.

👉 Click here and drop some linguistic love on Amazon. Or scan the QR code below

P.S. Remember that time when you were a wee little newbie in the vast world of languages? Someone out there is wearing those shoes right now.

Your words can be just the friendly nudge they need!

REFERENCES

Bertr, L. (2017, February 24). Listening - mastering one of the hardest parts of learning a new language. The Language Academy of the Carolinas. https://www.carolinalanguage.com/listening-mastering-one-of-the-hardest-parts-of-learning-a-new-language/

Best Reviews. (2022). StackPath. Bestreviews.net. https://bestreviews.net/how-to-learn-a-new-language-by-streaming-your-favorite-shows/

Clear Words Translation. (2017, November 21). Learning About Culture is Essential to Learning a Language. Clear Words Translations. http://clearwordstranslations.com/language/en/learning-a-language/

Craig, L. (2016, February 29). The Top 10 Tactics for Learning to Speak Any Language Fluently | FluentU Language Learning. Www.fluentu.com. https://www.fluentu.com/blog/how-to-speak-a-language-fluently/

D, S. (2015, April 8). How Do Children Learn Language? 4 Big Takeaway Lessons for Language Learners. FluentU Language Learning. https://www.fluentu.com/blog/how-do-children-learn-language/

Ertheo. (2018, November 27). Benefits of learning a second language at an early age | Ertheo Education & Sport. News about Soccer Summer Camps and Academies All over the World. https://www.ertheo.com/blog/en/learning-a-second-language/

Gkiokas, D. (2018, February 15). Why Adults Are Better Learners Than Children. The Metalearners. https://www.themetalearners.com/why-adults-are-better-learners-than-children/

Hammes, K. (2015, March 13). Three Quick Techniques for Speaking and Writing More in a Foreign Language by Fluent Language. Fluent Language Learning with Kerstin Cable. https://www.fluentlanguage.co.uk/blog/techniques-speaking-writing-foreign-language

Heerema, E. (2015, August 28). 9 Types of Mnemonics to Improve Your Memory. Verywell Health; Verywell Health. https://www.verywellhealth.com/memory-tip-1-keyword-mnemonics-98466

Idahosa. (2017, August 29). The 9 Biggest Myths in Language Learning - Busted. The Mimic Method. https://www.mimicmethod.com/9-biggest-myths-language-learning-busted/

Languages, O. (2017, September 20). The Importance of Speaking in Language

Learning. Ouino Languages. https://www.ouinolanguages.com/tips/the-impor tance-of-speaking-in-language-learning/

Languages, O. (2018a, January 9). What's the Hardest Part of Learning a New Language? Ouino Languages. https://www.ouinolanguages.com/tips/ques tions/whats-hardest-part-learning-new-language/

Languages, O. (2018a, January 9). What's the Hardest Part of Learning a New Language? Ouino https://www.ouinolanguages.com/tips/questions/whats-hardest-part-learning-new-Languages.language/

Languages, O. (2018b, March 7). How Can You Learn Languages with Netflix? Ouino Languages. https://www.ouinolanguages.com/tips/questions/can-learn-languages-netflix/

Languages, O. (2018c, April 25). How Many Words Can You Learn Each Day? Ouino Languages. https://www.ouinolanguages.com/tips/questions/many-words-can-learn-day/

Languages, O. (2018d, May 29). How to Turn Any Movie into a Language-Learning Tool? Ouino Languages.https://www.ouinolanguages.com/tips/questions/movie-language-learning-tool/

Languages, O. (2019a, October 29). Learning a Language? 4 Reasons to Stop Trying so Hard. Ouino Languages. https://www.ouinolanguages.com/tips/language-stop-trying-hard/

Languages, O. (2019b, November 14). The 3 Enemies of Language Learning (and how to beat them). Ouino Languages. https://www.ouinolanguages.com/tips/3-enemies-language-learning/

McCune, A. (2020, June 26). Why Mistakes are Important. Amy Sue McCune. https://amysuemccune.com/leading/why-mistakes-are-important/

Polizzi, M. (2018, February 5). They Speak Too Fast! 6 Active Listening Exercises for Learning a Language. Clozemaster Blog. https://www.clozemaster.com/blog/active-listening-exercises/

Richards, R. (2009, March 31). Making It Stick: Memorable Strategies to Enhance Learning Reading Rockets. https://www.readingrockets.org/article/making-it-stick-memorable-strategies-enhance-learning

The Intrepid Guide. (2021, March 19). 25 Tips for Procrastinators: How to Stay Motivated to Learn a Language. The Intrepid Guide. https://www.theintre pidguide.com/motivation-to-learn-a-language/

Warren, E. (2021, April 21). Memory Strategy: Hooking's a Fun and Memorable Way to Learn. Good Sensory Learning. https://goodsensorylearning.com/blogs/news/memory-hooks

Bright Hub Education website. [Online].[Accessed October, 2019]. Available from-World Wide Web: https://www.brighthubeducation.com/social-studies-help/

97047-importance-of-native-american-storytelling/ 2019 Bright Hub Education. All Rights Reserved.

ICAL TEFL website. [Online].[Accessed October, 2019]. Available from World Wide Web: https://www.icaltefl.com/good-news-bad-news

Pimsleur website. [Online].[September, 2019]. Available from World Wide Web: https://www.pimsleur.com/the-pimsleur-method 2011 - 2020 Simon & Schuster, Inc. Pimsleur® is an imprint of Simon & Schuster Audio, a division of Simon & Schuster, Inc. All rights reserved.v

Chris Shei, Monica E McLellan Zikpi, Der-Lin Chao (2020) The Routledge Handbook of Chinese Language Teaching: Creating a task based language course in Mandarin Chinese. Routledge, New York, NY, p.85

Eric Jensen (2005) Teaching with the Brain in Mind: ASCD Association for Supervision and Curriculum Development Alexandria, VA p.

Joe Winstonm (2012) Second Language Learning Through Drama: Practical Techniques and Applications, Routledge, New York, NY, p. 7

Mauro Morretta, Maria Grazia De Francisci (2014) The Learning Code: The Psychology of Total Physical Response: Linguistic Learning. Lulu Press, Inc.

Michael P. Berman (2011) English Language Teaching Matters: Teaching Idioms. O-Books, John Hunt Publishing, p.98

Nancy Bell, Anne Pomerantz (2015) Humor in the Classroom: A Guide for Language Teachers and Educational: Teaching With Humor. Routledge. p. 154

Paul Meara (2009) Connected Words: Word associations and second language vocabulary acquisition John Benjamins Publishing, Philadelphia, PA, p. X

Pimsleur, P. (2013). How to Learn a Foreign Language: Forward. Heinle & Heinle Publishers Inc., p.xiv

Richard Grünert (2009) Teaching English Through Songs: Skills Integration. GRIN Verlag. Druck und Bindung, Norderstedt Germany p.2

William Littlewood (1981) Communicative Language Teaching: Relating forms to meaning. Cambridge University Press, p. 8

Image by <a href="https://www.freepik.com/free-vector/brain-infographic-template-with-hand-drawn-items_1001536.htm#page=5&query=brain&position=44&from_view=search&track=sph >Freepik</a>

www.ingramcontent.com/pod-product-compliance
Lightning Source LLC
Chambersburg PA
CBHW051426130726
47987CB00005B/1938